MORALITY OF POWER

A NOTEBOOK ON CHRISTIAN EDUCATION FOR SOCIAL CHANGE

BY CHARLES R. McCOLLOUGH

A DOING THE WORD RESOURCE PUBLISHED FOR
CHRISTIAN EDUCATION: SHARED APPROACHES
UNITED CHURCH PRESS
PHILADELPHIA

Doing the Word resources are published especially for use in the denominations listed below:
Christian Church (Disciples of Christ); Church of the Brethren; Cumberland Presbyterian Church; The Episcopal Church; Moravian Church in America; Presbyterian Church in Canada; Presbyterian Church in the U.S.; Reformed Church in America; United Church of Christ; United Presbyterian Church in the U.S.A.; United Methodist Church

Library of Congress Cataloging in Publication Data

McCollough, Charles R   1934–
  Morality of power.

  (A Doing the Word resource published for Christian education)
  Bibliography: p.
  1. Christian education—Text-books for adults.
2. Church and social problems—Study and teaching.
I. Title.
BV1565.S6M3   261.8'07   76-56243
ISBN 0-8298-0329-7

Photos by Doug Magee

Scripture quotations are from the Revised Standard Version of the Bible, copyrighted 1946 and 1952 by the Division of Christian Education, National Council of Churches, and are used by permission. "Honeykill" on pages 36–38 is reprinted from "Honeykill: A Simulation" by Charles McCollough in *Colloquy,* July–August 1972. Copyright 1972 by United Church Press. Material on pages 135–37 is from *The Politics of Nonviolent Action* by Gene Sharp. Copyright © 1973 by Gene Sharp and used by permission.

This book is dedicated to my father and my brother, George W. McCollough, Sr. and Jr., poets, rebels, homesteaders; they never conformed beyond laughter.

ACKNOWLEDGMENTS

The exercises included here evolved over a three-year period in response to a need to discover the best way to educate for social change. They have been tested in a number of churches and conferences and have been influenced by a number of sources. John Westerhoff inspired the development of several of these exercises and concepts. Audrey Miller, the editor, especially encouraged the whole effort. Roseanne Giguere, Eugene Flug, Holly Henderson, Carol McCollough and a number of other friends contributed their ideas and support.

CONTENTS

FOREWORD

Charles R. McCollough has put the church and Christian education in his debt. Few issues in Christian education are as significant as the morality of power. While power may corrupt, the lack of power castrates. Power is God-given—a human right. But if power is to be blessed it is to be used on behalf of justice, liberation, peace, whole-community, and the well being of all. We cannot permit any use of power which oppresses others, nor support any social system which keeps people powerless.

Each and every person needs to be equipped with the knowledge and skills necessary to act for liberation, just as everyone needs to be aided in developing a capacity for moral thinking. Our understandings of power, our sense of our own power, and our ability to use power creatively, constructively, and morally are results of education. Born in the image of God, we humans are historic actors. Power is the ability to act. We have been granted by God the possibility of acting either for our own or God's purposes. Christian education needs to revive in us a sense of God's purposes and enable us to acquire the skills, sensibilities, and stimuli necessary to join God in God's history-making. Ultimately we are social beings. Personal and interpersonal actions are never sufficient. Only when we engage in social action do we complete and fulfill our humanness.

The *Morality of Power* is, therefore, a timely and essential resource to help congregations rethink and redesign their adult educational ministries.

Written in the honorable tradition of George Albert Coe, who, at the turn of the century, penned *A Social Theory of Religious Education,* Dr. McCollough has uniquely united theory and practice to provide the church with a much neglected perspective on education for social change.

Today, as never before, we are confronted by the challenge to make Christian education Christian. Typically, the aims and methods of Christian education are individualistic. We have forgotten that the redemptive mission of the church is nothing less than joining God in the transformation of the social order into the community of God. If Christian education is to be Christian it will need to be brought into line with this social message. Still, while Christian education is called to equip and stimulate us to live in the social world as followers of Jesus Christ, it more than likely teaches people about the Christian religion. Adult education in the church is typically the most escapist of all religious education, avoiding experience, action, and reflection and concentrating on information and thought about what the Bible says, what happened in the history of the church, what Christians believed or believe, and what is right and wrong. As a result, even when we have done a fair job of teaching people all about Christianity we have usually failed to enable them to be Christians. We have forgotten that Christian education is first and foremost *doing* the Word through four dimensions of learning: awareness, analysis, action, and reflection.

At long last, we have, in *Morality of Power,* a resource which provides strategies and educational designs for Christian social education. It is an honor and a privilege to recommend this unique collection of essays and exercises, theologically and ethically informed, and consistent with our best contemporary pedagogical insights. *Morality of Power* is an invitation to examine our current modes of adult Christian education and engage in the important and essential task of reforming the church's educational ministry. The challenge presented to us by this excellent educational resource is great. However, if it is used, it can aid in the transformation of both the church and society. Any takers? I hope so.

John H. Westerhoff III
Associate Professor of Religion and Education
Duke University Divinity School

PART ONE

INTRODUCTION

Morality of Power is for people who believe that Christianity can make the world a better place and who want to involve themselves in that task. This notebook is for those who wonder why the righteous and the innocent suffer while the wicked prosper. It is for those who refuse to accept injustice as the will of God. This notebook is for people who are broken by the cruel forces of society. It is for those who sense that God wants to help heal the sick, feed the hungry, and liberate the oppressed, but who are sometimes discouraged at the complexity of the problems, especially when their caring moves them beyond emergency relief to work on preventive solutions. It is for those who want to close the widening gap between the rich and the poor. It is for those who have caught a vision of the new world that could be if they joined God in its making.

This notebook is for educators who would prepare people for action and for activists who would educate others to be prepared.

A Notebook on Christian Education for Social Change has been created for leaders or enablers of youth and adults. It is designed to be used in church classes or at conferences and retreats. Many of the readings and exercises can be integrated in a variety of other educational programs as well.

Included in the text are two general categories of materials: educational exercises and background readings. In this way the notebook combines two critical fields of experiences, Christian education and social action—theory and practice.

The exercises are written with the enabler in mind. The procedures in each exercise give a step by step format to follow. A major portion of this book is devoted to stimulating and guiding immediately doable activities in which to test our thinking and behavior.

The other major part of this notebook is theory. The theory is in the form of background readings intended to make a few simple but helpful distinctions which should answer the most common questions one experiences in the church when working on social issues, such as, "Why do you mix religion and politics?" or "What does tax reform have to do with the Bible?" These essays should equip the layperson with answers that are clear, simple and convincing.

The essays are written and charted in such a way that the enabler of a class or a retreat can give a brief statement laying out the terrain to be experienced in the exercises. They can also be pulled out and given to people who want to examine the ideas behind the exercises.

The exercises and essays provide concrete experiences and interpretations for four levels of learning: affective, cognitive, active and votive.* Educational experts insist that learning should include all of these levels. Really to know something is to feel it, think it, act on it and sense its value.

The structure of this book relates these four levels of learning to match three basic steps in

---

*These four levels of learning are discussed further in the following pages.

social action: that is, assessing the desirability or undesirability of social conditions, projecting and designing alternatives for the undesirable conditions, and using power morally to change those conditions. This is getting a bit abstract; so let us look at it through the recent experience of people involved in Christian social action.

Expanding the Dimensions of Learning

In the civil rights movement, many educators and social activists tended to follow the greatest educator of them all, Socrates. It was assumed that to *know* the good was to do the good, so educational programs were set up to enlighten those people (both Blacks and whites) who behaved as though Blacks were inferior. For Blacks, more integrated education was sought; for whites, more enlightenment about the equality of all people was preached. Sit-ins involved Blacks and/or whites, with Blacks sitting and waiting for long periods in segregated restaurants. They were almost never served. It was thought at the time that poor education was the problem. Obviously, education as knowledge was needed, but it would not have been enough. If a waitress or waiter had been enlightened and had served the Blacks, they would have been fired.

After realizing this, the movement went back to the drawing board and developed the idea of "interracial dialogue." The problem was defined as a lack not only of knowledge but of feelings and interpersonal relations as well. As one young white person said, "I have never shaken the hand of a Negro." That was the clue to the problem, it was thought. Get Blacks and whites together in small groups to work out their problems and develop more "brotherhood." "Take a Negro to lunch" was a motto in some white groups. White churches began to try to have small meetings and meals with Black churches across town. Interracial dialogue began. Knowledge was supplemented by the small-group approach to develop good feelings and the findings of group dynamics were very helpful.

This interpersonal approach did develop small-group dialogue, but the problem remained. Blacks were still treated as second-class citizens even when there was enough "knowledge" of this injustice and even when there were genuine feelings of "brotherhood." In one such dialogue group, a Black man said that the *structures* of the bank for which he worked were such that whatever correct knowledge or affirmative attitudes people had, the bank—and even the Black himself in his position— would still discriminate against Black people in the loan department.* In other words, structures and social roles were still a problem even when inadequate knowledge and bad feelings were overcome. So back to the drawing board again.

Without rejecting the need for accurate knowledge and good small-group relationships, an even broader approach had to be found that dealt directly with social structures. So *action* was added to knowledge and small-group process, and educational programs were developed to include cognitive, affective, and active levels of learning. Activists criticized education without action as only a "head trip." An action and reflection model began to be used.

Christian activists had a special problem: to act in a way that was different from the usual application of power politics. Recognizing that structures of power must be dealt with and that the usual procedure was to confront and defeat them by amassing more power, Christian activists needed an alternative that would avoid this win-lose approach. Was there not a way for everybody to win in a win-win arrangement? The issue became: How do you deal with corrupted power structures without becoming corrupt yourself? The problem is not one of uncorrupt people beating corrupt people. Corruption infects us all. "For we are not contending against flesh and blood [people] but against the principalities, against the powers [Eph. 6:12]." That is, our efforts are against corrupt structures which lock in both the people who benefit from them and those who are oppressed by them.

In response to this difficult problem, some people went back to more and more affective learning in small-group encounters. Others went for power, defending the use of power politics with the question, "If the ends don't justify the means, what does?" Force field analysis was used: a procedure that sought to increase the countervailing forces and to neutralize or decrease the prevailing forces—same weapons, different constituency. This was done in the civil rights movement, in urban training, in draft resistance and the peace movement in general, in the labor movement, and in the corporate respon-

*See Reuben A. Sheares and S. Garry Oniki, *Next Steps Toward Racial Justice* (Philadelphia: United Church Press, 1974), for a more detailed record of racial justice problems.

sibility effort. In extreme cases, activists became so political that it was hard to distinguish them from their opponents.

One does not have to choose between using power politics and ignoring the problem of needed structural change, but the middle ground is very hard work. Many people had exhausted themselves in social action campaigns. (They were so intense, so unpredictable, and required such massive exertion that one's energy, perspective, and values easily became depleted.) Many civil rights and peace activists therefore eventually turned inward and joined rural communes or esoteric religious cults in order to restore their energy and perspective.

So once again, some of us went back to the drawing board to find out what religious educators knew all along: You can't ignore your spiritual needs or spiritual expressions of the divine reality for very long before your world becomes unglued and your creative energy stops flowing. Therefore, we needed to consult our religious traditions and practices and add the votive level to the affective, cognitive, and active levels of educational practice.

The votive level of learning is concerned with the religious devotions people experience. It works at the level of one's values, faith-commitments, and ultimate concern. We learn at the votive level through activities such as reflection, prayer, singing, artistic expression, dance, worship, and ritual of various kinds. Reflection is used here in a special sense, meaning a process of meditation, contemplation, dialogue and evaluation. When we reflect on an action, we reevaluate our behavior from the perspective of our deepest commitments and values as well as from that of our visions and plans for action in the future.

Our experience over the past two decades confirms the need for learning at all four levels: affective, cognitive, active, and votive. Educators can design methodologies for working at all four levels of learning as their contribution to education for social change.

The educational methodology of Doing the Word is the AAAR process.* This process has four components: awareness, analysis, action, and reflection. Each component includes all four levels of learning, but one of the levels is usually em-

*This book is primarily a leadership resource for Doing the Word, one of the four approaches in Christian Education: Shared Approaches, a project of Joint Educational Development.

phasized more than the others in each component. Thus, in stimulating awareness, more attention is paid to the feeling or affective component; in the analysis component, the cognitive level is emphasized, while in the reflective component, the cognitive and volitional levels tend to be more predominant.

This methodology is based on and can be related to the work of social activists as well as educators for social change. Let us examine some contributions in this area of educators and activists to see how they are combined for effective social change.

Combining Education and Action

Kurt Lewin, a sociologist, named the process of social change very simply many years ago. He identified three simple steps: unfreeze, move, freeze.

First, the social conditions (racial or sex discrimination, militarism, political corruption, or economic exploitation) have to be made fluid—that is, they have to be questioned and declared unacceptable. They must no longer be taken for granted, accepted as fate, natural, unchangeable, or normal. People have to become conscious of their social conditions as the result of historical decision rather than natural determinism. Instead of being satisfied with their slavery in Egypt, for example, Moses had to create dissatisfaction and discontent among the Hebrews. The absolute, frozen tyranny of Pharaoh had to become fluid. Paulo Freire calls this unfreezing step in which oppressed people become aware of their place in nature and society, conscientization.

Such awareness leads to discontent with oppression and the desire to move out. This is the second step, moving toward an alternative land of milk and honey. Conscious awareness of one's social condition and its arbitrary historical nature leads to dreams of alternatives, of another authority or god, a better life, a dream or vision of a new land for freedom and justice, a New Jerusalem. Through planning, preparing, training, and building, the necessary means for escape are developed. The move toward freedom takes place. Power is employed. An alternate life begins.

But reestablishment in a new land takes as much effort as the escape, and the freed slaves must learn how to use the power of self-government. The group must take the third step of freezing a new social order.

There are, of course, many more intervening factors in a liberation movement, whether it is the Exodus story, the American Revolution, African liberation, Black liberation, or women's liberation. But the essential ingredients are discontent with the present social conditions, a vision of an alternative system, and the exercise of power to change that condition. So one can summarize the social-change aspect of our task as social conditions, alternatives, and the use of power. As regards social structures, the social activist can share knowledge and experience in these three areas. But in order to do education for social change thoroughly, there must be educational methodologies by which we can gain awareness of, knowledge of, ability for, and commitment to change the social conditions, see the alternatives, and use power. That is, a blending of education and action.

Educators contribute the valuable tools that start "where people are." Social activists seek to move people to where they want them to be. The educator asks what people *need;* the activist says, "What is the *task? What is to be done?"* Educators hope to change people. Social activists hope to change structures.

We must constantly ask both "What is the need?" and "What is the task?" and ask within the context of the religious question, "*Why* are we needing and doing it?"

What are the needs and the tasks in the context of our ultimate religious values? If we keep juggling these three balls (the need, the task, and the values) at the same time, we will be able to educate ourselves and others for changing the structures of power, and do so without using the weapons of power politics. Educators understand the needs of people and how to communicate directly to those needs. Social activists know how power works and how to pull the right lever at the right time. Both seek to empower others rather than themselves. Both enable others to know and to act. Both stay in the background and coax and challenge others to become as enlightened and as strong as they can become. Christian values give direction to both. *Christian* educators who do the hard job of combining these two fields of education and action with a Christian value system will know how to change unjust social structures in a way where everybody wins. This is our utopian goal. It is our vision. It is a difficult one to attain, but we can move toward it, depending on God to give us the power (grace) to do so.

Thus the task of the educator is to create the conditions for maximum awareness, knowledge, ability, and commitment to the terms of social structure which we have summarized in three words: conditions, alternatives, and power. Under each interface there are subtasks: for example, awareness of social conditions requires such things as (1) enabling the experience of discontent with social conditions, (2) enabling the experience of these conditions as a problem, and (3) enabling the experience of these conditions as changeable.

Now, there are educational exercises to help people discover how to do these tasks. This is the basic framework of this notebook. The following graph illustrates this schematically.

A Schema for Defining
Christian Education for
Social Change

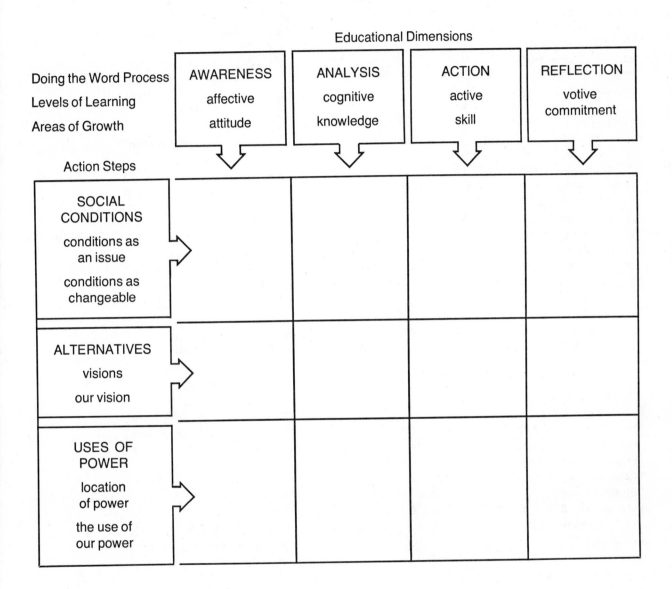

Educational Dimensions

	AWARENESS affective attitude	ANALYSIS cognitive knowledge	ACTION active skill	REFLECTION votive commitment
Doing the Word Process / Levels of Learning / Areas of Growth				
Action Steps				
SOCIAL CONDITIONS conditions as an issue / conditions as changeable				
ALTERNATIVES visions / our vision				
USES OF POWER location of power / the use of our power				

AAAR LEADERSHIP SKILLS

What would a person skilled in Christian education for social change look like? It is important to be as clear as possible about our educational goals in this effort, so we have defined very specific techniques that are needed to accomplish the intent of the four components of the AAAR process: awareness, analysis, action, and reflection.

It is helpful for the enabler and the participants in the AAAR educational method to test their competencies in these areas. That is, ask "What would I be able to do if I were skilled in Christian education for social change?" The following questionnaire is intended to help people answer that question. It might be used both at the beginning and at the end of the study/action course, as one means of evaluation.

It should be noted that this is an ideal listing and does not assume that any one person could have all or even most of these skills. But everyone already has some of them, and to identify these is the purpose of the questionnaire. It is also helpful to identify all the skills and abilities resident within the whole group so that their efforts together can complement each other.

PROCEDURE

Read the following statements and consider each as it relates to your skills. Then circle the number, on a scale of 1 to 5, that represents the way you feel about your competence in that specified area. From the top of the scale, 5 represents a high degree of ability; 3 represents satisfaction with your skills but with recognition of a need to improve; 1 represents a need to be compensated in this area.

I. IN THE AREA OF AWARENESS

A. I am skilled in *consciousness raising* because . . .

   Low   High

1. I have the ability to help create openness toward diversity in attitudes, life-styles, assumptions, life experiences, and insights of groups other than our own.   1 2 3 4 5

2. I am able to raise critical probing questions about social conditions.   1 2 3 4 5

3. I am able to build rapport with oppressed groups of people.   1 2 3 4 5

4. I am able to facilitate dialogue between representatives of oppressed groups and church groups.   1 2 3 4 5

5. I am able to focus feelings of discontent on a definable problem or set of problems which can be affected by action for change.   1 2 3 4 5

B. I am skilled in *building intentional community* because . . .

6. I can apply the insights and methods of effective group process within my church group.   1 2 3 4 5

7. I am able to build relationships between and within coalitions of church and community groups.   1 2 3 4 5

8. I am able to help church people identify as members of larger social groups related to specific social issues.   1 2 3 4 5

C. I am skilled in *gaining social perspective* because . . .

9. I am able to perceive individual facts, events, and experiences within a context of interrelated social facts and influences (i.e., I see the "interconnectedness" of events rather than "events in isolation").   1 2 3 4 5

II. IN THE AREA OF ANALYSIS

A. I am skilled in *understanding social conditions* because . . .

1. I am able to articulate social problems, perceive their structural parts and their interrelationship, and help others to do the same.   1 2 3 4 5

2. I am able to point people toward reliable sources of information.   1 2 3 4 5

B. I am skilled in *building visions of alternatives* to the status quo because . . .

3. I am able to point to existing alternatives as a stimulus for the group's imagination.   1 2 3 4 5

4. I am able to encourage and inspire creative fantasizing within groups. 1 2 3 4 5

C. I am skilled in *understanding the nature and use of power* (including the unique power of the church) because . . .

5. I am able to create situations in which my group can discover our own power(s). 1 2 3 4 5

6. I am able to point a group toward available information on the nature and uses of social power and to lead probing discussions of the questions raised. 1 2 3 4 5

III. IN THE AREA OF ACTION

A. I am skilled in *planning* because . . .

1. I am able to help a group in goal-oriented thinking, in identifying aims, potential resources, alternate strategies, etc. 1 2 3 4 5

B. I am skilled in *organizing* because . . .

2. I am able to help a group identify its potential constituency for joint work on a given problem. 1 2 3 4 5

3. I am able to foster effective communication, coalition building, and planning between the church group and its broader constituency. 1 2 3 4 5

C. I am skilled in the *execution of plans* because . . .

4. I am able to be logical with a sense of appropriate timing (i.e., I have a practical sense of necessary sequence and the timing of specific actions within a plan). 1 2 3 4 5

5. I have good interpersonal skills of communication and empathy to reduce friction within the action group and to minimize the resistance of those whom they hope to influence for change. 1 2 3 4 5

6. I am able to raise a group's energy level when needed. 1 2 3 4 5

7. I have the ability to be careful about details. 1 2 3 4 5

IV. IN THE AREA OF REFLECTION

A. I am skilled in *evaluating action experiences within a religious context* because . . .

1. I can help members of the group identify the feelings and insights they experienced during the action and those they have now as a result of it. 1 2 3 4 5

2. I am able to help a group relate the experience to the Bible and to theological perspectives. 1 2 3 4 5

B. I am skilled in *gaining religious/social identity* because . . .

3. I am able to help individuals clarify their personal values and beliefs. 1 2 3 4 5

C. I am skilled in *affirming* and *celebrating* the new level of insight and *commitment* because . . .

4. I can help a group find fitting symbolic and ritual expression for its spiritual experience, values, and commitment. 1 2 3 4 5

5. I am able to use nonverbal as well as verbal expression for the votive-level meaningful experience (i.e., music, art, ritual, drama, dance, etc.). 1 2 3 4 5

Ranking Group Skills and Needs

It is important to say again that this is an ideal listing of leadership skills related to the AAAR method. There is no expectation or promise that one or all can acquire the twenty-seven skills listed here by faithfully reading the essays and doing the exercises. But one can expect that using the notebook will (1) identify what skills are present individually and collectively, (2) provide a refresher course for those who have the skills but for whatever reason have not used them fully, and (3) indicate the skills needed to continue Doing the Word (responding to God's vision for a new world) through awareness, analysis, action, and reflection.

Procedure for Ranking

1. Collect the responses of the individual participants.

2. Record the total markings for each of the statements on the following chart under the appropriate number from 1 to 5.

3. Study the chart, celebrating the skills present in the group and identifying areas of need.

4. As plans are developed for education for social change, the information on this chart should guide planners and enablers. If plans are already completed, the information here might indicate a need to rearrange or modify those plans. It is important for the group to have exercises and experiences that make them feel good about who they are and what they *can* do, as well as experiences which help them identify what yet needs to be done and attempt to meet that need.

Evaluation

If the questionnaire is used before the course or program begins, keep the original sheets for use as one means of comparison and evaluation. If the time together will be long-term, evaluation might occur periodically. If shorter, there should be an evaluation at the conclusion.

I. AWARENESS

A. Consciousness Raising — Low ... High
1. Create openness toward diversity — 1 2 3 4 5
2. Raise critical, probing questions — 1 2 3 4 5
3. Build rapport with oppressed groups — 1 2 3 4 5
4. Facilitate dialogue with diverse groups — 1 2 3 4 5

B. Discontent
5. Translate feelings into solvable problem — 1 2 3 4 5

C. Building Community
6. Apply methods of effective group process — 1 2 3 4 5
7. Build coalitions — 1 2 3 4 5

D. Gaining Social Perspective
8. Identify with larger social groups — 1 2 3 4 5
9. Perceive "interconnectedness" — 1 2 3 4 5

II. ANALYSIS

A. Understanding Social Conditions — Low ... High
1. Articulate social problems and their structural parts — 1 2 3 4 5
2. Know reliable sources of information — 1 2 3 4 5

B. Envisioning
3. Recognize existing alternatives — 1 2 3 4 5
4. Inspire creative envisioning (dreaming) — 1 2 3 4 5

C. Recognize Power
5. Facilitate discovery of a group's power — 1 2 3 4 5
6. Know the nature and uses of social power — 1 2 3 4 5

III. ACTION

A. Planning
1. Lead in goal-oriented thinking — 1 2 3 4 5
2. Identify potential constituency — 1 2 3 4 5

B. Organizing
3. Foster effective communication — 1 2 3 4 5
4. Be logical, with a sense of timing — 1 2 3 4 5

C. Implementing
5. Use interpersonal skills — 1 2 3 4 5
6. Stimulate energy — 1 2 3 4 5
7. Be careful about details — 1 2 3 4 5

IV. REFLECTION

A. Evaluate Action
1. Identify feelings and insights — 1 2 3 4 5
2. Relate experiences biblically, theologically — 1 2 3 4 5
3. Clarify personal values and beliefs — 1 2 3 4 5

B. Celebration
4. Find fitting symbolic and ritual expression — 1 2 3 4 5
5. Use verbal and nonverbal religious expression — 1 2 3 4 5

USING A NOTEBOOK ON CHRISTIAN EDUCATION FOR SOCIAL CHANGE

This book is composed primarily of educational exercises which demonstrate the awareness, analysis, action, reflection (AAAR) process and essays or readings which further develop the underlying theory of the exercises. In addition, two other auxiliary sections have been included: the Supportive Resources and Selected Bibliography.

In order to facilitate use of this notebook, a word about each of the five sections follows, as well as some illustrations of how one might plan programming for Christian education for social change.

Exercises

The exercises are grouped according to the AAAR pattern, which can be entered at any point. They are paired, with awareness/analysis in one exercise and action/reflection in another. These two pairs of exercises are linked to make a complete AAAR pattern. However, one should dip in at one's point of readiness, recognizing that all four steps in the process are critical to Christian education for social change.

Long, detailed games that require elaborate explanation and additional hardware have been avoided. Board games and expensive equipment are also excluded. It is intended that these exercises be simple and stimulate people to create their own (see pp. 21–22).

Background Readings

The exercises fall into three main groupings: social conditions, alternatives, and the use of power.

Each grouping of exercises is followed by background readings that explain the theory supporting the exercises. The readings are written on a strictly cognitive level. While it is not essential for all participants to read the essays, they will be helpful to many and should definitely be studied by the enabler. Simple graphs and charts are provided for the enabler to use in getting the point of the exercises across. But in each case, the experience precedes the reading to ensure an inductive learning process. As in all aspects of the book, the background readings can be pulled out and used independently. Their purpose is limited but important. They provide a conceptual framework for the rest of the material.

Supportive Resources

Part Three of the table of contents lists twenty-one Supportive Resources that are referred to in various exercises. Some of these resources are suggested for use in more than one exercise and some have many more possibilities than the exercise suggests. Therefore, they are gathered in one section to facilitate locating them. Unlisted supportive resources are limited to the exercises in which they appear.

Bibliography

The bibliography is a selective and limited list of books related to the practice and theory of the content of this notebook. The list is intended to develop further the ideas contained here as well as identify several of those whose ideas were germinal to the exercises and readings designed for this notebook.

Additional information and curricular resources related to the AAAR method used in Doing the Word, Christian Education: Shared Approaches can be obtained by writing to the educational department of your denomination listed on page 2.

Programming Notes

These exercises assume that the people who use them have a personal religious commitment but have not made a firm connection with the social implications of that commitment. However, they assume that youth and adults are not likely to read long essays on theology, ethics, or economics, but that they will commit a limited time to a well-structured learning experience, such as six or seven one-hour-a-week sessions or a long retreat weekend. Such a format only permits the use of a small portion of the exercises. Under these circumstances one should select two exercises from each section such as (from Section I) "What's *Your* Problem?" and "What's *the* Problem?"; (from Section II) "Visioning the Good World" and "Visioning Independence"; and (from Section III) "Winners and Losers" and "Planning for Hope." This will give people a taste of Christian education for social change.

It is hoped that more time would be available, however, in which to experience more exercises and discuss the background theory. There is enough material here to last for as many as twenty-four two-hour sessions, should it be possible to engage people for this period. In such a case, the group could simply move through the notebook from front to back, using one exercise per session for the first hour or one hour and a half and then discussing the accompanying reading for the second hour or hour and a half. The book is organized in such a way that the first exercises stimulate persons to thinking about social conditions and then to moving to action on their own social problems.

WEEKLY SESSIONS

A more likely arrangement is a shorter time period in which the group can pick and choose which exercises and background readings and supportive resources to use. Many combinations are possible. For example, The Gas Meter and Spotting Power Politics are adaptable for use in most exercises. They can be used with other supportive resources as well as with any other arrangement the group chooses.

It is essential to have an enabler or coordinator of the sessions. Someone needs to hold the group together and move the learning experience along. This role can be passed around if necessary, but someone must organize the group and announce the procedures. It is expected that the enabler will read all the material and be ready to explain the procedures clearly and carefully.

At times, the readings and the supportive resources will need to be duplicated for each participant. For example, the Cardinal Rules for Making Change (page 138) can be given to the group after they sense a clear need to have such a list. In every case, inductive learning (that is, having the experience of a need before the solution is given) is preferable.

If weekly sessions are chosen, the enabler should begin each session with a very brief (ten minute maximum) explanation from the background reading related to the subject of that session. The exercise can then be used according to the procedures in each. This can be followed by discussion and application to the group's own experience. The enabler should not only limit her/ his speeches, but any long-winded monologues given by dominating members. It's the enabler's job to call cloture on all filibusters.

A WEEKEND RETREAT

Participants should always be encouraged to apply the learning in the community and become active on social concerns. Ideally, weekly church meetings could become the reflection part of an action/reflection life of a congregation. If a weekend retreat is planned, besides reserving a location and other logistics, retain a Third World or minority person to speak on the Saturday night of the retreat.

The format for a weekend retreat might be arranged as follows:

Friday
6:30—7:00 Arrival, registration, settling in
7:00—8:00 Introduction, get acquainted, and general explanation of purpose, using material from Section I, Background Readings on Grasping the Social Conditions

8:00—9:00	Any awareness/analysis exercise from Section I
9:00—9:30	Wrap-up and brief celebration
9:30—10:00	Snacks, informal singing, discussion

Saturday

8:00—9:00	Breakfast
9:00—10:00	Any action/reflection exercise from Section I
10:00—10:30	Smoke and beverage break
10:30—12:30	Any set of two exercises together from Section I
12:30—1:30	Lunch
1:30—2:30	Private reading in background material and meditation
2:30—3:30	First half of the visioning exercise from Section II, Envisioning Alternatives
3:30—4:00	Smoke and beverage break
4:00—5:30	Second half of the visioning exercise from Section II
5:30—6:30	Free
6:30—7:30	Supper
7:30—8:30	Lecture from a guest out of a dependent background, such as a Third World country or a minority group. It is important that such a person be conscious and articulate about social conditions in her/his background
8:30—9:00	Discussion with guest
9:00—10:00	Films and reading
10:00—10:15	Celebration and snacks

Sunday

8:00—9:00	Breakfast
9:00—11:00	One pair of exercises from Section III, Using Power
11:00—12:00	Back-home planning (What do we plan to do when we return?); election of a continuing steering committee
12:00—12:30	Worship service
12:30—1:30	Lunch and departure

Follow-up plans made at a retreat are very important. See that a steering committee representing the group meets within three weeks to plan follow-up and additional educational and action plans.

The exercises and readings included here can be used in a variety of other ways in addition to those suggested. They can be supplementary pieces to other courses of study. They can be redesigned within the framework of existing curriculum, for example, confirmation study. They can be incorporated into the study/action program around a particular issue or in the development of certain skills. The materials are designed to be flexible. The notebook format is intended to encourage readers to pull sections out and rearrange them for their own purposes.

DESIGNING EDUCATIONAL EXERCISES

One of the most useful contributions this notebook can make is the way it inspires others to initiate their own education and action efforts. Educational exercises are like physical exercises. They are all a matter of practicing in low-risk situations (with the right amount of challenge and support) what you want to do in the high-risk life situation. This notebook intends to encourage the reader to create individual educational programs and exercises, because the closer the educational experience is to the life situation of the participant, the more learning takes place.

Many of the exercises in this notebook can simply be adapted to fit the issues most relevant to the users. Nothing is sacred about their form or content. So read through them and substitute more immediate concerns for the ones presented. After using a few of the exercises included here, try your hand at inventing one. Note the form these exercises follow:

1. Purpose: What do you intend to accomplish?
2. Assumptions: What facts do you assume are required for this exercise?
3. Preparation: What does the enabler need to do before the exercise is used?
4. Time: How long will it take?
5. Materials: What physical props are required?
6. Procedures: What steps are to be taken?
7. Supportive Resources: What data or educational designs will help?

We have found that these are the essential ingredients in a good exercise. Here are a few more suggestions for creating and enabling your own:

1. Get to know the particular social condition well so that the basic issues are dealt with.
2. Help people to create a nonrisk learning environment to strengthen them for real-life action, for example, to role play or simulate the issues and some of their possible solutions.
3. Keep it simple and limited to small, doable issues.

4. Be very clear and precise about procedures.
5. Keep the personal, interpersonal, and social dimensions included in the experience.
6. Encourage *group* participation in the discussions and dialogues. Encourage shared use of the airwaves.
7. Provide clear questions and limited, manageable problems that challenge people's knowledge and experience without overwhelming them.
8. Provide warm, friendly support and a familiar, affirming atmosphere without boring or smothering people.
9. Always discuss the experience afterward and encourage people to summarize their own learnings.
10. Combine private study with group discussion and action.
11. Include affective, cognitive, active, and votive as aspects of the exercises. Having all four levels provides balanced and integrated learning.
12. Start where people are, but by all means don't end there.

One final word to the enabler: Be sure to look over all the material in a section beforehand, including the background readings. If participants will read, be sure to make the readings available to everyone. Become familiar with the procedures in each exercise and be ready to coach participants in their various roles. Recognize that adults have very little time and a short attention span, not because they are less intelligent but because they are more occupied with daily hassles. So make it interesting and brief and current and relevant to their experience.

Finally, social change will not occur if we seek either to *destroy* oppressive people or to *help* oppressed people. Our job is to learn how to live and work and behave as brothers and sisters (equals) confronted with common principalities and powers and structures that temporarily benefit a few at the expense of many. These social structures, rather than individual people, must be *changed* so that all people stand equally before God.

PART TWO

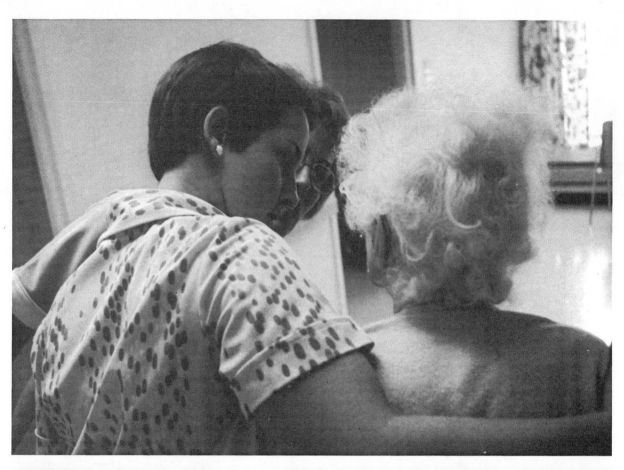

I. GRASPING THE SOCIAL CONDITIONS

OVERVIEW

The exercises in Section I are designed to initiate people into thinking, feeling, and acting on problems from a large-group or social perspective. They seek to help people see that past experiences and Bible stories, normally interpreted on a private level, can also be seen to have a social dimension.

"What's *Your* Problem?" and "What's *the* Problem?" are simply exercises that clarify and enforce the distinctions between community problems as seen on personal, interpersonal, and large-group levels. "What's *Your* Problem?" employs a role play with a psychiatrist, a group process expert, and a community organizer to "solve" the problems on each level respectively; "What's *the* Problem?" uses a community interview. Games Pharaohs Play is a Bible study that helps people discuss the tactics of power politics. Checking Out the Pharaohs applies it to the present time with a Gas Meter gauge. The pair of exercises dealing with givens and changeables seeks to help people gain the wisdom to know the difference between what one can change and what one must accept. Auction is a priority-bidding exercise that helps people reflect on their values, work together, and make hard choices. Honeykill is a simulation of a church experience in which a set of global and local issues are brought together in realistic church committee and congregational meetings.

These exercises are fairly elementary. But this is intentional because they are written for folks who have not viewed the issues with eyes that see the whole social and moral dimensions of these common problems. The veteran of education for change should be able to see through the first few.

The three readings which follow this set of exercises are intended to support the learnings and experiences therein. They are meant to amplify further the discoveries and new understandings, or to reinforce and enrich what one already knows.

Some of the readings or essays are referred to directly in the procedures of one or another exercise. When this happens it would be best to read the essay at that time. It is essential for the enabler to read all of the essays in preparation for leading the exercises. It would be helpful to make copies available for participants whenever possible or desirable.

Where essays are not directly referred to in the exercises, the topics are such that connections between the two are clear, for example, the relationship between the exercise What's *Your* Problem? and the essay Distinguishing Large-Group Behavior is easily recognizable after one has read or experienced the exercise.

EXERCISES IN GRASPING SOCIAL CONDITIONS

WHAT'S *YOUR* PROBLEM?   **PART 1 AWARENESS/ANALYSIS**

PURPOSE:
To stimulate awareness and enable analysis of a problem from a social perspective.

ASSUMPTIONS:
We rarely see a daily problem from a social perspective. Most often our day to day hassles are viewed as private problems for which we blame ourselves or people nearby. The ability to detect social causes and consequences of a problem is critical in education for social change.

PREPARATION:
Read through the exercise. Decide which problems are to be used. Choose the people to play the three roles carefully, particularly the role of the community organizer. Provide the time they need to get into their roles. Provide clues, techniques, and values in each role for the three who will role-play.

TIME:
1 hour, approximately

MATERIALS:
Room with movable chairs and tables
Copies of suggested problems
Copies of role-play directions
3 x 5 cards
Newsprint and marker

PROCEDURE:
1. Ask for three volunteers to play one each of the following roles:
    psychiatrist
    group process expert
    community organizer
   Give each their role-play directions.
2. Ask for two or more observers who will distinguish the differences between the ways problems are perceived.

3. Give to each of the other group members one 3 x 5 card with one of the suggested problems on it.
4. Each person with a problem goes to the psychiatrist, the group process leader, and the community organizer in turn. The problem solver asks each person, "What's your problem?" The problem is stated, an analysis is offered, and the player goes to the next expert. *(30 minutes)*
5. In plenary session observers report distinctions between each response. These are recorded on newsprint. Those with problems should also comment on distinctions they observed. The role players should have an opportunity to express how they felt in their role. *(15 minutes)*
6. Further discussion can relate other daily problems that have personal, interpersonal, and social-group aspects. Help people to ask their own questions and to seek alternative solutions. *(15 minutes)*
7. If this exercise is to be followed by Part 2, "What's *the* Problem?" take time now to explain next steps, i.e., do #1 to 5 of procedures for "What's *the* Problem?"

ROLE-PLAY DIRECTIONS
(Type or duplicate, cut and paste on separate 3 x 5 cards.)

> Psychiatrist: You see all problems as personal, individual ones whose origins are in early childhood development. Whatever problem it is you diagnose and treat as early childhood fixations.

> Group Process Leader: You see all problems as interpersonal difficulties between individuals. Solutions are, therefore, better communication and dialogue between these individuals.

> Community Organizer: You see all problems as a struggle between large groups of people, institutions, and social structures. Some have all the power, others none. Your solutions are, therefore, to transfer the power.

SUGGESTED PROBLEMS
(Type each on a 3 x 5 card; include other local problems if you wish.)

> 1. You just lost your job at the shoe factory.

> 2. The union is picketing your office and you are afraid to cross the line.

> 3. You are mad at the obese people you see on TV demanding more food stamps.

> 4. Your grocery bill is double last year's!

> 5. You just read that the millionaire heir to a cosmetic fortune paid no taxes last year.

> 6. You are angry that your daughter is joining the army.

> 7. Your children's school will close two months early for lack of funds.

WHAT'S *THE* PROBLEM?

PURPOSE:
To experience the way community leaders interpret community problems and to reflect on those responses.

ASSUMPTIONS:
It is helpful to have constant encouragement to make the distinction between personal and social problem solving.
Action in our community and reflection in our learning group are means to providing that encouragement.

PREPARATION:
Be prepared to untangle the social aspects of problems from their personal and interpersonal aspects.

TIME:
If this exercise is done independently of "What's *Your* Problem?" you need to plan to do it in two parts: first, to give instructions and assignments *(30 minutes)*; second, to report in and reflect *(1 hour)*.

MATERIALS:

Two cardboard boxes, one smaller than the other.   Paper, pencils
Newsprint, markers   Copies of A Biblical Litany: Visions and Strategies

PROCEDURE:
1. Have the people pair off into action teams.
2. Present a sample list of problems, such as:

    Drug abuse in community   School taxes
    Automobile and industrial pollution   Hunger
    Unemployment   Racial strife
    Vandalism   Local church refuses to ordain or call a woman pastor
    All-male city council

3. Have each team select one of the problems listed or one of their choice not listed.
4. Ask teams to call three community leaders (a political figure, a business person, and an educator) and ask these leaders to give their views on the causes and solutions to this problem. They might take a copy of the Gas Meter with them.
5. Immediately after the interviews each team writes down the responses and analyzes them as to the personal or social perspective assumed by the community leader.
6. When the total group reconvenes, have each team share its report. On newsprint, chart responses from each team by categories of personal, interpersonal, social.
7. Have the group analyze the problems and offer a solution on all three levels.
8. Have each person write down a list of personal problems that have been seen from a purely personal perspective.
9. These lists are then placed in the small box labeled "My box of worries" in the middle of the room.
10. Take the small box and hold it over the larger box labeled "Global village" as a prayer is recited. The prayer might be one of petition, asking God for wisdom and insight and reminding us of our interconnectedness.
11. Place the small box in the larger box. Have the group form a circle with the "Global village" box in the center.
12. All join in the litany.

SUPPORTIVE RESOURCES:
A Biblical Litany: Visions and Strategies (pages 112–13)
Gas Meter (page 115)

PURPOSE:
To enable people to see that the Bible offers insights on social as well as personal problems.

ASSUMPTIONS:
It is seldom observed in Bible study that many of the social problems we have today and the way people handle them were dealt with long ago in the Bible. Moses' responses to Pharaoh give us some clues about our own behavior toward present day tyrants.

PREPARATION:
Read Three Approaches to Religious Issues, keeping in mind that you want to avoid tangled interpretations of biblical form criticisms and long sermons.

TIME:
1 hour

MATERIALS:
Old Testament for each person
Newsprint and markers or chalkboard and chalk
Three Approaches to Religious Issues

PROCEDURE:
1. Briefly explain the three different approaches to problem solving—personal, interpersonal, intergroup—and the way these color our interpretation of the Bible. (See Supportive Resources: Three Approaches to Religious Issues.)
2. Divide the group into research teams of two to five people and ask them to research Exodus 5:1-22 with the following questions in mind: *(30 minutes)*
   a. Name the social conditions in Egypt.
   b. List the specific actions Pharaoh took to quell the potential rebellions, such as discredit leadership, divide and conquer, blame the victim, etc.
   c. List solutions you would have used to counter Pharaoh's action.
3. Have groups select convenor and reporter.
4. In a plenary session each team should report their findings. The report can be listed on chalkboard or newsprint in three columns: Conditions, Pharaoh's Acts, Possible Solutions. *(20 minutes)*
5. Continue discussion, focusing on groups that are today in a similar position to Pharaoh and the children of Israel.
6. If this exercise is to be followed by Part 2, Checking Out the Pharaohs, you might do #1–4 of that exercise now. They are preparatory experiences, and it would be much more effective to have a fresh experience than try to recollect a past event. (The participants will need copies of the Gas Meter.)

SUPPORTIVE RESOURCES:
Three Approaches to Religious Issues (page 114)
Gas Meter (page 115)

CHECKING OUT THE PHARAOHS

PURPOSE:
To act and reflect on the ways rulers stay in power.

ASSUMPTIONS:
After the awareness/analysis exercise, studying Exodus in Games Pharaohs Play, it is useful to apply these insights to present day realities in an action/reflection exercise.

PREPARATION:
Duplicate copies of the Gas Meter for each participant. Read Exodus 14:5-30. Prepare the water pans and have some people in the group ready to initiate the singing and dancing. Think about an appropriate closing benediction.

TIME:
1 hour, approximately

MATERIALS:

Bible	Large pebbles
Paper, pencils	Copies of Gas Meter
Two pans of water	Timbrel or small hand-drum

PROCEDURE:
1. List persons or institutions with a dominating influence in your life (past or present), such as an employer, a military figure, an organization head, a teacher, an economic group, a racial group.
2. Plan a meeting with that person or a representative of that institution (or recall such a meeting in the past and write it down).
3. If such a meeting is arranged ask for this person to explain some policy of that institution which you feel is unjust. Take notes on this response. (If you are recalling this meeting, recall the typical response you received.)
4. Rate this response on the Gas Meter provided.
5. Meet with a subgroup of three persons and reflect on this experience. Further develop your list of techniques that rulers use to stay in power and see how this affects you and your friends. *(15 minutes)*
6. In plenary session discuss these responses. Note similarities and differences. *(15 minutes)*
7. Then have individuals crush their paper lists around one of the pebbles and walk between the large containers of water marked "Red Sea," dropping in (washing away) the tyrannies of Egypt.
   While the members are "passing through the waters," have one member read Exodus 14:5-30. After they all drop in their lists they might sit and reflect on the passage.
8. After five to seven minutes of silent meditation and after all have passed through the "Red Sea" to liberation, all rise and dance and sing with timbrels. Use songs like "Oh Freedom," "Go Down, Moses," "We Shall Overcome." *(30 minutes)*
9. End session with a benediction.

SUPPORTIVE RESOURCES:
Gas Meter (page 115)

GIVENS AND CHANGEABLES

PURPOSE:
To help people begin to distinguish what is given from what is changeable in social conditions on an awareness/analysis level; to help people think in social categories as distinct from personalistic categories.

ASSUMPTIONS:
People often do not distinguish social conditions that can be changed from given realities that cannot be changed. Distinguishing them is helpful for problem solving and issue analysis.

PREPARATION:
Think over the distinctions between givens and changeables. Read Distinguishing Large-Group Behavior in Background Readings.

TIME:
1 hour

MATERIALS:
Questionnaire on page 32 can be duplicated, one for each participant
Room with movable chairs
Pencils
Newsprint and markers

PROCEDURE:
1. Briefly explain meaning of givens and changeables. Givens are necessary, immovable realities of a social situation. Changeables are not necessary or inevitable and can be changed. *(5 minutes)*
2. Pass out questionnaire for individual answers. *(10 minutes)*
3. Designate two areas in room, one area marked for "Givens" and one for "Changeables." Two signs will do.
4. People should vote with their feet by walking to "given" side or "changeable" side as leader reads the items aloud one by one. *(30 minutes)*
5. Allow one and one half minutes' discussion among people after each vote, for people to explain why they made the choice they did.
6. Final session is a general summary discussion. List on newsprint the "givens" and "changeables." List other "changeables" that may seem to be "givens." *(10 minutes)*
7. Suggest that people be conscious about daily problems after the session and consider whether the situations are given or changeable.
8. Report back findings at next meeting.

Prayer
God grant me the serenity to accept the things I cannot change
Courage to change the things I can and the wisdom to know the difference.

—Reinhold Niebuhr

Questionnaire for Givens and Changeables

Check "Given" those things you believe are unchangeable and inevitable in our society, and check "Changeable" those things you believe are passing, changeable phenomena which are not necessary.

	Given	Changeable
1. Death at old age		
2. Taxes		
3. Drug abuse		
4. Capitalism		
5. Cancer		
6. Progress		
7. Industrial and automobile pollution		
8. Vandalism		
9. The profit motive		
10. The strongest will survive		
11. The sovereignty of God		
12. War		
13. 8 percent unemployment		
14. Inflation		
15. Equal opportunity		
16. Masculinity/femininity		
17. Love		
18. Institutions		

REAL GIVENS AND IDEAL CHANGEABLES   PART 2 ACTION/REFLECTION

PURPOSE:
To act out the distinction between givens and changeables and to see how the realist and the idealist see them. To reflect on Jesus' approach to given realities and changeable ideals.

PREPARATION:
Have a clear picture of each role assignment and be prepared to coach each player on the distinctions. Duplicate role assignments. Have an area set aside where the three can work into their roles.

TIME:
1 hour

MATERIALS:
Bible
Attached role assignments
Room for role play
Room for meditation

PROCEDURE:
1. Set up role play. Ask for three volunteers to play the roles of Jesus, realist adviser, and idealist adviser. Ask for volunteer observers to respond to the role play. Give actors their role cards. *(10 minutes)*
2. Have "Jesus" and his advisers huddle to get into their roles. *(10 minutes)*
3. Describe the setting: Jesus goes into the wilderness to pray, to discuss the will of God, and to receive empowerment and wisdom. He is concerned about his mission in relationship to occupied Palestine. He is concerned about the plight of the people he has just left: their hunger, their oppression, their imprisonment. He studies Isaiah. He knows he must do something. The issue is *how* to do it.
4. Advisers then come to "Jesus" to give advice on how to:
   a. Deal with hunger and poverty
   b. Deal with political power
   c. Deal with convincing the people (his style of communication) "Jesus" responds to each. *(15 minutes)*
5. Observers respond to the differences they hear. The enduring wisdom of Jesus: how practical is it? how idealistic? how wise? What meaning does this have for us: individually, collectively? *(20 minutes)*
6. Then, "Jesus" goes into the sanctuary or a room set up like a church/synagogue. Everybody follows him and sits down. He opens the Bible to Luke 4:1-20 and reads very slowly, substituting "I" (first person) for "he" and "Jesus" (third person), for example, "Full of the Holy Spirit, I returned . . ."
7. After five minutes of silence, "Jesus" says, "Today, this scripture has been fulfilled in your hearing."
8. Concluding prayer and benediction.

Role Play Assignments

REALIST ADVISER
You always advise that people accept the real given situation. "Be realistic" is your slogan.

You are hard-nosed and very suspicious of starry-eyed dreamers who get people hurt by naive actions.

You assume all groups in society and all nations are out to take all they can get unless stopped by another power.

You advise that the only real options are working with the power forces that exist. You would "balance" them to achieve as much as you can of your goals.

The facts are your people are dominated by a ruthless Roman militia and religious leaders who cooperate with them.

IDEALIST ADVISER
You always advise people to look for a change for the better. "Be idealistic" is your slogan.

You are softhearted and very worried about ruthless realists who don't flinch at violence and shady "deals."

You assume that all groups in society and all nations will take only what they need if the process of love and concern is given a chance.

So you advise that working with the present power arrangements must be avoided.

"JESUS"
You want to do something about the poor and hungry, to release prisoners and liberate the oppressed.

You are undecided about details of how to do it.

You're tempted to be (1) a bread winner, (2) a political/military messiah, or (3) a magic worker.

You answer these with: (1) "People need more than bread," (2) "People need more than politicians," (3) "The liberating and healing power of God cannot be controlled by our whims."

AUCTION

PURPOSE:
To give people an opportunity to rank values related to social justice. To realize the different priorities found within a group and to work for group consensus.

ASSUMPTIONS:
World resources are unequally distributed. This is a problem and is changeable.

PREPARATION:
Select an auctioneer. Allow time for the auctioneer to get in the role.

TIME:
30 minutes

MATERIALS:
Copies of Auction Items for each participant

PROCEDURE:
1. Divide group into subgroups of four to five people. Each group gets 150 denarii with which to bid.
2. Have each group choose a bidder and come to consensus as to what this person will bid for in their name. Items will be auctioned off in the order in which they appear.
3. After auction:
   a. Determine which items people spent the most for. This might indicate a priority.
   b. Have each individual list in order his or her top three. Compare with (a) above.
   c. Discuss reasons for priorities. Reflect on: can we do anything now to bring some of these priorities into reality? What? How?

Auction Items

_____ All health care and medical needs guaranteed for your lifetime

_____ A job for your family sufficient for basic needs

_____ Freedom from violent and criminal actions (mugging, theft, murder, rape, etc.)

_____ The right and ability to do what you want to do when you want to do it for ten years

_____ Some guaranteed leisure time every day of your life for reading, relaxing, worship, or whatever you choose

_____ Honesty and competency in elected officials in government

_____ An integrated world in which racial barriers to job, educational, and housing opportunities are destroyed

_____ A world without civil and international wars

_____ A world in which all nations have equal access to natural resources on a per capita basis

_____ Freedom from anxiety plus good emotional and physical health for you and your family

_____ Guaranteed income of $100,000 per year for life

_____ Equal opportunity for a meaningful education for all people

PURPOSE:
To show how a church can begin to struggle with overcoming large issues and local problems.

ASSUMPTIONS:
This simulation assumes that local churches are affected by and can, in turn, affect large issues, that education is most successful when real or simulated decisions are being made, and that acting out these decisions in a simulation helps equip people do so in real life situations. It also assumes that large corporations have a crucial influence on a community's economy, its jobs, and even its moral and spiritual attitudes.

PREPARATION:
Read over profiles and be prepared to manage each step of the simulation, keeping time and leading the evaluation discussion at the end.

TIME:
2 hours
Mid-September

1. Introduction	10 minutes
2. Group caucuses	15 minutes
3. Board meeting	20 minutes
4. Group caucuses	15 minutes
5. Congregational meeting	30 minutes
6. Evaluation	30 minutes
Total	2 hours

(allow longer time for larger groups)

MATERIALS:
Profiles attached

PROCEDURE:
1. Introduction: Enabler introduces the simulation, reviewing the aims and setting an informal atmosphere based upon the rationale provided. Divide into groups and distribute profiles.

2. Group Caucuses (I): People are divided into five groups. If there are only six people, each can represent one group. When each group meets, they are to read the description of the town, the church, and Honeykill Corporation. They decide on how they will act at the church board meeting, at which, it is known, the youth group will make some demands.

3. Church Board Meeting: The youth group presents its demands to the board and asks the board to support these demands at the congregational meeting where the final decision is made. Each representative of a group should seriously act out the attitude one would expect in real life—decisions that persons in the church might make. The chairperson of the church board should take up the demands along with other typical church business of the church meeting. All groups may attend the board meeting, but of course, only the board can vote. (All people can vote at the congregational meeting.)

4. Group Caucuses (II): Whatever is decided at this board meeting will affect the outcome of the final decision at the congregational meeting. Here, the youth group asks the whole church (or a majority vote) to support its demands. A second strategy caucus is called so each group can organize its approach for the congregational meeting in the light of the board meeting.

5. Congregational Meeting: This is conducted by the board chairperson. Discussion and voting of the whole group on issues ensue.

6. Discussion and Evaluation of Simulation: Now the total group is asked to relate this simulation to the situation in its own church. Some suggested questions are:
   a. What decisions were made?

b. How did people feel at particular points?

c. What could have happened to change the outcome?

d. How similar were the meetings to your own church situation?

e. How can we bring world issues to our local church's concern?

f. Who makes the most important economic decisions in our community?

g. Are jobs and companies in our community dependent on war production? If so, how can this be changed?

7. End with prayer and singing hymns.

Profiles: Groups

1. Board of Deacons and Minister: The board members are aware of the youth group's demands before the board meeting and have to plan their response in light of the overall good of the church. Only they vote at the first meeting to which others come with concerns. Of the twelve members, seven have teenagers in the youth group.

2. Youth Group: These young people have been studying the Honeykill Corporation and are disturbed by its military, South African, and other activities. They have come to their church with the following demands:

a. The church should sell off all 200 shares of Honeykill stock;

b. The church should request that Honeykill should leave South Africa;

c. The church should stop letting Honeykill use the church's parking lot;

d. The chairman of deacons should resign from this job or from Honeykill because Christian church concerns are inconsistent with war and apartheid profiteering;

e. The church should ask Honeykill to hire 10 percent Black employees (instead of the current 2 percent), with 5 percent in executive positions.

3. Blacks in Church: All the Blacks are very concerned about Honeykill's hiring practices and South African involvements. But many are concerned about reprisals against them if they speak up. So they do not voluntarily back the youth group at the meeting. But they'd like the youth group to get its demands to the total church.

4. Christian Education Committee: Some want to share the youth group's concerns, but most of the committee tends only to support a study course on Honeykill Corporation for senior high students and adults. Permission may be asked of deacons for such a course of study.

5. Deacons: No agreement with the youth. Made up mostly of executives with Honeykill. They believe such issues should not be discussed in church and that to bring them up will divide the church and destroy it economically.

Profiles: Community and Institutions

(Duplicate six of these profiles, one for use in each group.)

PROFILE OF SPRINGFIELD, "HOME OF HONEYKILL"

Population—50,000:
60% Protestant
30% Roman Catholic
10% No affiliation
70% Northern European ancestry
10% African ancestry
20% Southern European ancestry (most recent)

Politics:
55% Republican
35% Democrat
10% Independent and unregistered

Economics:

A one-industry town dominated by the Honeykill Corporation and its executives. Almost everyone works for Honeykill, with the exception of a few retail merchants, some professional people (lawyers, doctors, teachers), and a small group of wealthy retired people.

PROFILE: FIRST COMMUNITY CHURCH

800 members
250 attend regularly
1 Minister
1 Director of Christian Education
6 Black families
Mostly young, up and coming engineers and business people

Church politics:

$85,000 budget
Sanctuary paid for but there is a new religious education building debt of $65,000
Pastor retires in ten years
A new, recently graduated director of religious education interested in issue education and social change
Youth Group: highly politicized with the help of the new director of religious education.
Chairman of board of deacons is executive director of Honeykill.
Six of the twelve deacons are executives with Honeykill and one is on Honeykill's board of directors. The chairman of the board of directors contributed over $50,000 to the Republican Party in 1968 and is the largest contributor to the church, with the chairman of the board of deacons.
Church has $30,000 endowment and owns 200 shares of Honeykill Common.
Stock worth $10,000.

PROFILE: HONEYKILL CORPORATION

Products:

Basically electronic, but has acquired a number of other companies, such as a textbook company and a home appliance company.
Makes various missiles: air-to-air and ground-to-air, and has large contracts to make MIRV missiles for Trident submarines. Makes computer components at plant in South Africa.

Sales:

55 percent of sales are to the military. This amounts to about $550 million a year.

Plant:

Built by government at taxpayers' expense. Springfield Division is one of a number of Honeykill plants. Springfield Division deals with communications and ordnance. Plant was provided with 3 million tax dollars' worth of equipment which Honeykill uses (for both military and commercial production) rent-free.

Employees:

Some Honeykill scientists also work for colleges in area. Many secretaries, assembly line, and janitorial workers. Almost all are women or of African or recent Southern European ancestry. Honeykill provides the jobs. "What's good for Honeykill is good for Springfield."

Connections:

Board of directors has many interlocks with banks, technical universities, and communications industries. There are two ex-military, high-ranking naval officers on the board of fifteen men. There is a Honeykill information office in Washington, D.C., to keep tabs on military contracts and to work on the state's legislative delegation to ensure defense appropriations to the state and thus to Honeykill.

BACKGROUND READINGS ON GRASPING THE SOCIAL CONDITIONS

1. THE LARGE-GROUP POWER MACHINE

The exercises in this section are intended to help people become actively conscious of the different ways of perceiving and acting that are necessary in large groups, as contrasted to small groups and individuals. They assume that we seldom see our daily problems as having social dimensions, much less distinguish the different kinds of solutions called for in each realm.

We will go about sorting out the differences between groups and individuals like Adam did sitting in the garden one day: naming the beasts. If we can name some of the "beasts," maybe we can tame them. If we can tame them, maybe we can make our garden a better place to live in.

The beast that we are talking about here might be called the "large-group power machine." To name small groups we need to know something about it, how it works, or what it does. For instance, most leaders know what small groups are. Members come together and separate. They develop leaders. Small groups have an understandable way of functioning, so ministers and other small-group leaders understand and *name* these functions. Then they know how to make small groups function to get something done rather than just sitting around the committee room, shaking heads and reading minutes.

We have also learned a lot about how individuals function; what causes depression, what can be done for alcohol and tobacco addicts and people with other personal obsessions. These personal problems are still rampant, to be sure, but we can at least know their names and a few prescriptions for spiritual cures.

What we have not really named to this point is the "large-group power machine." Instead of being like a small group of people, this large group contains and controls a large number of people in a group, such as rich people, poor people, Black people, white people, and so forth.* We know a little about how small groups work. How do big ones work? What "games" do they play? Psychologists tell us that individuals run on *eros* (life force) as their driving motivation. Some behavioral scientists tell us that small groups of people seek *philia* (brotherly/sisterly love), but large groups are driven by *power*. If we can understand power within the context of theology, we can name and maybe tame this huge beast. We can get a grasp of the large group and how it works and understand how morality is related to power. We can distinguish the moral uses of power from power politics.

We have modernized many of our present day beasts and monsters. Dragons and ghosts no longer scare us much. We now call our beasts machines. We don't worry any more about animals

---

*By large groups, is meant a socially defined grouping which usually refers to a large number of people, but sometimes the group may be small in number but large in power, such as a dictator. Both are large groups from a perspective of function and social power.

overpowering us now like we used to. Rather, we worry a lot about machines running us over—eating up our energy and our green grass, putting us in debt, polluting our air, and finally doing us all in by drinking the last drops of our precious oil which is running out, or by blowing us up in one last blast of a doomsday machine.

It's silly, of course, to talk about a machine that actively "drinks" or "hurts" passive people. Machines don't have souls or wills or make decisions like people do. So why be afraid of machines? Because even though machines don't have independent minds that intend to do us in, many people think they do. No, many people *behave as if* they did. You will remember that it was not a real live beast that did in the children of Israel in the wilderness. Rather, it was a "work of man's hands," a sacred golden cow that did the trick. In the same way the large-group power machine, although it's made by the work of people's hands, gets out of control because we let it mystify or spook us. We *behave as if* it were a deciding, all-powerful person. So this big machine goes on overpowering groups of people, including us. We think it is our fate to accept or adapt to the way one group pushes around and runs over another group. Since it is often difficult or impossible to find a real live, mean individual to blame for all this, we give up and say it's hopeless to resist, so we adapt.

It is possible, however, to name, understand, and do something about large groups the way we have named and understood, and even helped individuals and small groups. Unfortunately, people very often confuse the structure of individuals with that of large groups and vice versa. For example, an individual may be depressed and the prescribed remedy may be the presence of trusted friends. But a large group does not get depressed. A large group gets oppressed. Like the outcasts throughout history, a large group of people like the Israelites needs the staples of life: food, safety, energy, shelter, jobs and hope. When these are denied, the people are oppressed. Unfortunately, most people do not prescribe food, safety, energy, shelter, jobs, or hope to help other groups out of oppression. No, most people, especially religious people, see a group of outcasts and offer them instead something that helps cure individual depression rather than large-group oppression. Many times when well-intentioned people see a group of people starving or run off their land, they are moved by moral compassion to help. So what

do they do? They do what they know how to do; they try to help the way they would help a depressed individual, by being friendly to, say, American Indians or foreign students or the elderly or Blacks. But it does only limited good.

We have to respect these good intentions. But the problem is that we rarely apply morality to the big groups or understand how the big groups function. The result is that good-intentioned people are like the well-meaning first-time voter who left a message in the ballot box saying, "God bless you all." That is not bad personal morality. It just does not make much difference to the large-group power machine. If morality for the individual is motivated by conscience, and morality for the small group runs on love, we can say that large groups are motivated by a morality of power.

We said that most people simply adapt to the large-group power machine and say, "That's life." But not all people adapt. Some people learn just enough about it to make it work for them and against others. The big machine does not care who it runs for; it just grinds along uncaring and often independent of everybody. The people who know a little about running the machine are often called the "winners," and the people who get gobbled up are the "losers." Everybody else is a middle echelon slave to it because they don't think the machine is people-made and can be changed by people. For this reason, the few people who know the machine get more than anyone else, and, therefore, they like to perpetuate the mystification about the machine. They say "You can't change it," "God meant it this way," "It will all fall down if you protest," and other fearful sayings. For instance, the winners of religion said this in medieval times to the losers, but the losers finally stood up and said, "Well, maybe so, but let me read the Bible myself and just see if what you winners are saying is true." A little later the political winners, feudal kings, and princes and their attendants said the same thing about the political order: "You can't change it." "God made it this way." "It will all fall down." And other fearful sayings. Again, the losers stood up and said, "Well, maybe so, but let us decide that with a representative government and we will see if it all falls down."

Now the winners who run the large-group power machine today say, "You can't change the present social/economic structure; God meant it that way. If you tamper with it, it will all fall down." But slowly and surely, the losers are beginning to rise up and say, "Well, maybe so, but let us decide. We want the basic staples of life: food, safety, energy, shelter, jobs, and hope. Then we will see if it all falls down." "No," say the winners, "you will not have the incentive to work for the big machine if you are given all the staples of life." The middle-echelon people who just barely get along agree, saying, "Don't mess around with the big machine. It may not be perfect, but it's all we got."

Now what the losers are trying desperately to find out is the secret of how the machine works, so they can keep it from overpowering them. This, of course, is very hard to do, because they have been taught to worship and serve the large-group power machine, too—even to fight and die for it, if necessary. The losers nearly always believe that the machine is sacred. So they cooperate with their own slavery to this sacred cow or machine, even as it eats up the last bit of food from their plates.

The secret is that the large-group power machine is just a person-made machine. It is neither sacred nor God-given, and certainly not good enough to eat up our food and gobble up the losers. When this secret is let out, the world will not fall. We will all become winners.

2. DISTINGUISHING LARGE-GROUP BEHAVIOR

Now let us take a closer look at the large-group power machine and see how it functions. Individuals, small groups, and large groups function differently but they have three things in common. Each has a basic structure, a set of barriers to fulfillment and a set of solutions for overcoming the barriers. The Bible did not separate individuals from groups. People were classed in tribal or national groupings. Jesus is introduced, for example, as being "in the lineage of David." The Bible assumed human structures. Barriers and solutions applied to both individuals and to large groups. The basic structure of humans for Paul was a kind of spiritual battlefield where law and flesh were at war. As people fought between legalism and temptation of the flesh, the Lord sent the spirit to overcome both. "For the law of the Spirit of life in Christ Jesus has set me free from the law of sin and death. For God has done what the law, weakened by the flesh could not do: . . . he condemned sin in the flesh, in order that the just requirement of the law might be fulfilled in us, who walk not according to the flesh but according to the Spirit [Rom. 8:3-4]."

Individual Perspective

This is Paul's three-point doctrine of people, which he wrote about to a group of Christians in Rome. It applies to individuals, small groups, and large groups. Unfortunately, in modern times we have almost exclusively limited our interpretation of law, flesh, and spirit to our psychological interpretation of isolated individuals. Our view of these aspects of people parallels closely Freud's superego (law), id (flesh) and ego (spirit). We "see" the Bible through the glasses Freud has put on us. So we read it in a very private way. Graphically it looks like this:

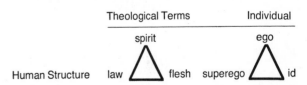

In order to distinguish the way large groups function, it is helpful to consider some current popular psychological perspectives. The purpose of mentioning these psychological terms is not to teach psychology but merely to form a bridge from where we are to an understanding of large-group behavior.

After Paul, the church went on to list a number of barriers that keep people from God. That is, when the law of the flesh ruled, people sinned. The seven deadly sins were lust, pride, gluttony, sloth, covetousness, envy, and anger. These were the barriers people must overcome in life, or else—off to the fires of Hades. In psychology they were not called sins, but many barriers to psychological health were named; they were called ego defense mechanisms, such as delusions of grandeur, projection, overcompensation, introjection, rationalization, or regression, put up to avoid facing reality. In the church, sins were overcome by the grace of God in a process that varies somewhat, but generally included (1) a vision or revelation of God's glory as compared to our sinfulness, (2) a confession of guilt, repentance and conversion, (3) remorse and determination to change, and then (4) a living out of the "new man"* in a sanctified life.

Psychology isolated individuals in a doctor-patient relationship and recommended a solution that involved an analysis of an individual's past, a facing up to his or her present real world, and a mental health treatment for the future. Following a medical model, classical Freudian psychology sought out childhood fixations and, through transference to and beyond the psychoanalyst, brought the "patient" out of childhood fixations to a mentally healthy adult life. Here is a graphic comparison:

	Theological Terms	Individual Perspective
Human Structure	spirit / law △ flesh	ego / superego △ id
Barriers	Sins	Ego defense mechanisms
Solution	Revelation Confession Salvation Moral life	Overcome defense mechanisms

Small-Group Perspective

More recently psychology has been expanded into social psychology and the behavioral sciences. Here we observe people not in isolation, as early psychologists did, but in small groups of two, three,

or a dozen. There are many theories about small-group behavior. One popular and very helpful theory is found in transactional analysis, which sees the basic structure of people always in immediate relationships where one person is transacting with another.

Instead of assuming that people are constructed out of law, flesh, and spirit, or superego, id, and ego, transactional analysis observes that people behave in their interactions either as a parent, a child, or an adult in any one transaction. All are appropriate in general, but in particular transactions one behavior (either parent, child, or adult) is most appropriate. If one behaves as a child when the parent response is more appropriate or vice versa, the transaction fouls out—that is, the people in the exchange begin to "play games." These games have been named the "games people play," such as, "ain't it awful," "why don't you," "yes, but," "rapo," etc.*

The solution to overcoming the barriers in transactions involves learning how to detect the games, learning how to have appropriate transaction where one's "child," "parent," or "adult" responds at the right time. To continue our graph, it looks like this:

Theological Terms	Individual Perspective	Small-Group Perspective
Human Structure		
spirit / law △ flesh	ego / superego △ id	adult / parent △ child
Barriers		
Sins	Ego defense mechanisms	Games people play
Solution		
Revelation Confession Salvation Moral life	Overcome defense mechanisms	Learn appropriate responses of child, parent, adult

Another recent small-group application of psychology is assertiveness training. One author has outlined human behavior in relation to other people as either flight, fight, or assert.† When challenged by other people, we do often bounce

*Language which refers to male and female will be *quoted* in the traditional pattern, but sexist language will not be used in the text itself.

*See Eric Berne, *Games People Play* (New York: Grove Press, 1964) and Thomas A. Harris, *I'm OK, You're OK* (New York: Harper and Row, 1969).

†See Manuel J. Smith, *When I Say No, I Feel Guilty* (New York: Dial Press, 1975).

back and forth between fleeing or fighting without ever learning how to respond creatively by asserting our rights and needs in a firm but controlled way. Assertiveness training helps one to detect one's particular flight-or-fight pattern or barriers to affirmative relations in small groups of people. The training helps develop a program of self-assertion.

This very brief summary of these approaches is meant only to illustrate some of the present assumptions behind the way we can and often do interpret and apply biblical insights. The wisdom of psychology and social psychology is extremely helpful in giving persons a framework and practical help in dealing with one's self. This can be expanded to be even more helpful, however, if we ask the same thing of large groups of people. How do we behave most appropriately toward a large group of people? What structures can help us begin to understand them? What are the barriers to positive intergroup relations? What are some solutions to overcoming these barriers?

Large-Group Perspective

When it comes to understanding the behavior of large groups, people often throw up their hands in bewilderment saying, "I've got enough trouble just getting along with my parents, friends, kids or neighbors. Don't put the whole country on me." So understanding large groupings—how they are structured, the basic barriers that keep them fighting each other—is either ignored or left to the police officers, generals, and politicians who do worry about large blocks of people.

However, the behavior of large groups of people can be understood just as that of individuals and small groups can. A few simple terms can be used for doing just that, so we can sort out some of the broad limits of education for social change. Large groups of people behave in certain structural ways; they erect barriers to positive behavior between groups, but they also find solutions to overcoming these behaviors.

It is helpful to observe large groups of people (for example, male, female, Black, white, elderly, youthful, white-collar, etc.) as having a structure just as individuals and small groups do, but it is not the same structure as superego, id, and ego, nor is it a parent, child, and adult relationship. It is more helpful to observe a relationship between large groups as one of either *dominance, dependence,* or *interdependence.* We often observe how one group, such as a nation, declares independence from another *dominating* nation. We are well aware of how males have dominated *dependent* females as a group of people. And we are rapidly becoming aware of the necessary *interdependence* of all people on the limited food and fuel resources of the earth.

One group may dominate another group for decades or centuries, as the Soviet Union dominates Central Europe, or as the colonial powers dominated Africa and most of Asia, or as whites have dominated Blacks in the United States. This domination has many unhappy consequences, but its most basic feature is that it causes dependence by the group that is dominated. This happens by two basic means: the dominating power makes all the crucial decisions for the dependent group, and it makes the rules for the dependent group. This dominant/dependent relationship is self-supporting. For example, the dominant male and dependent female encourage each other in these roles, even though both limit their full human and spiritual development by this relationship. The man who says to the woman, "Don't worry your pretty little head, I'll take care of it," is affirming his dominant role of deciding and rule making. The woman who says, "Oh, *you* do it, I can't. You're such a big, strong man," is affirming her dependent role of giving in to male domination and manipulating the man on a more subtle level. Both dominance and dependence, like Paul's law and flesh, are lesser human qualities. These relationships are of the "law of sin and death." They are "controlled by the flesh," to use biblical terms.

Now when the dominant/dependent relation exists between groups, it is very difficult to change, not only because the dominant group members (for example, the Egyptians over the Hebrew slaves in the book of Exodus) do not want to "let my people go" but also because the dependent slaves prefer the "fleshpots" of Egypt to "freedom in the wilderness." Moses had as much trouble keeping the children of Israel revved up to escape as he did outsmarting the Pharaoh and his magicians. So it was with Gandhi in India and Martin Luther King, Jr. in the United States and with all other prophets and liberators. The Pharisees, Sadducees, and soldiers were no more a problem to Jesus than his own followers, who were falling asleep, betraying him, and often missing the point. Dominance and dependence need each other. It takes two to tango. It takes a slave for there to be a master. It is a symbiotic relationship.

Games Pharaohs Play

Now there is an almost endless list of games pharaohs play or clever ways the slaves try to return to the fleshpots of Egypt. The Bible and the church list many of the barriers as sins, and psychologists have listed many ego defense mechanisms people use as games people play. What are some of the barriers larger groups erect to protect their dominant/dependent relationship and to avoid interdependence? That is, how do large groups block the development of interdependent relationships between groups? How do they subvert the effort to full human freedom of people who should have a say in all the decisions and rules that govern their lives? We will discuss some of these in a later section on the use of power (see pp. 79–109). Here we can point out a few barriers which we can call social-control mechanisms. The two most important are Slavery's Normal or That's Life, and Deciders Rule or Follow the Leader.

That's Life and Slavery's Normal are expressed in phrases like "You can't fight city hall" or "What's the use?" The point is that dominant/dependent groups use this mechanism to protect the status quo and to avoid rocking the boat. The pharaohs always insist that slavery is normal, God-given, natural, fated—an unquestionable arrangement that cannot and should not be changed. The slaves suffer under this arrangement, but repeat over and over to each other, "That's life." It is the first control mechanism because if slaves never question the worth or horror of slavery, they will never be liberated. What Moses did first of all was to say, "Slavery's not normal. Pharaoh is not God. No, Yahweh is the only God." To say that God is God is the most radical statement anyone can make because it says all human powers, kingdoms, and nations are relative and mere passing temporal structures that come and go. It abolishes the fatalism of a "that's life" attitude. It says slavery is not normal; it is a sin, a desecration of God's children. All people are equal because God is the only one who decides and rules our lives. No other group or person can dominate another if God is in charge. No group can cling to slavish dependence if there are no other gods before Yahweh.

But, of course, slaves and masters don't always listen to the prophets. And where prophets show up, promising liberation, they are often run out of town by the dominant groups—and the dependent groups as well. And the prophets are dumped in the garbage heap at the edge of town, the people are mumbling to one another, "Don't rock the boat," "Slavery is normal," "That's life."

A second set of barriers to interdependence can be called Deciders Rule or Follow the Leader. This social-control mechanism is very simple but also very subtle. One of the most prevalent features of dependence is the inability to make decisions and the inability to order and rule one's life. Dependent groups often prefer to "follow the leader." Likewise, a dominant group, by its nature as dominant, makes all the vital decisions and rules that control a large group or groups. Dominant groups not only fill a void created by the dependent group's indecisiveness, they also arrange it so that the dependent group can't make important decisions or rules.

For example, the people in a company town live in constant fear of losing their jobs, because they have become dependent on their jobs and thus on the company that hires and fires them. But occasionally a company will be found to have unsafe working conditions, or to be polluting the town water or producing bad products. When confronted with the challenge (from Ralph Nader, for example) that the plant produces cancer-causing material in the air or water, what are the workers going to do? They usually protest. "Why, this is awful. It could ruin the whole town." But these cries are *not* against the company. No, they are against prophet Nader, whom they run out of town while they are mumbling "Don't rock the boat" because their jobs are threatened.

Now the company representative steps in and innocently asks the workers, "What are we going to do? If we stop pollution, you lose your jobs. Now you don't want that, do you?" "No, no!" they shout. "Give us pollution." ("Give us Barabbas.") The pollution continues and so does the dominance/dependence because no one asks the central question: Who is making the decisions and who is setting the rules and options by which we are made dependent?

In this case the decisions are made by the company. It decides whether the plant will stay open or lay off or close down. It sets the narrow range of options for the dependent choice: work or no work. The workers, of course, decide one thing. They decide to remain dependent on the company and suffer the pollution. But the real decisions that control their lives remain with the company.

This approach is not only a classic picture of a mill town from the nineteenth century. It happens over and over when defense contracts are sought by companies, whether or not the weapons are necessary. The options are not given a worker (or even, in some cases, the company, in the present conditions of the military-industrial complex) to decide about the merits of a weapon. The options are only a contract or no job. Being dependent on the job, the workers and the company lobby furiously for the weapon. "Never bite the bullet that feeds you" is the motto. The issue remains: Who decides, who rules, who follows, who sets the options? Whoever makes the decisions rules the day. Whoever makes the rules writes them so he or she will make the important decisions. Likewise, whoever depends on this arrangement will keep handing over the decision-making to the ruler and following the leader.

These social mechanisms are two barriers to interdependence. Many others like pedestal, blame the victim, and protection will be spelled out later. For now, this is enough to indicate the structure and barriers that determine the way large groups function. But just as the Bible uses certain words for describing the solution to sin, and psychology has shown various processes for solving the defense mechanisms and games people play, we can suggest some processes for solving the problems of dependence/dominance.

How do you get to an interdependent relation between large groups? The classical means is violent revolution, in which the dependent group overthrows the dominant group and throws them into slavery or simply kills them off. There must be a better way. There is a better way.

We mentioned in the Introduction how various methods of change take place, whereby a dominant/dependent status quo is unfrozen, moved, and "refrozen" at a different level. The steps were summarized earlier as (1) becoming actively aware of the present social conditions, (2) envisioning alternatives, and (3) exercising power to achieve those alternatives. Our attempt here has been to open up the realm of the large-group consciousness and show how it can be understood and worked on in the same way that individual and small groups can.

Now we can complete our graph to include the categories of the large group:

	Theological Terms	Individual Perspective	Small-Group Perspective	Large-Group Perspective
Human Structure	spirit △ law / flesh	ego △ superego / id	adult △ parent / child	interdependent △ dominant / dependent
Barriers	Sins	Ego defense mechanisms	Games people play	Social control mechanisms
Solution	Revelation Confession Salvation Moral life	Overcome defense mechanisms	Learn appropriate responses of child, parent, adult	Consciousness of social conditions Vision of alternatives Power to change

We are trying here to begin where people are. We assume that theological terms are important but very fuzzy to most people. We also assume that psychological terms are well known and understood by most people. Building on these assumptions, we are seeking to move to the next step by showing that, first, *large-group behavior is understandable and changeable;* second, *our basic roots in the Bible apply to large groups as well as small ones and individuals;* and, third, *we affirm education that provides learning about all three groupings, i.e., individuals, small groups, and large ones.* None can be ignored even as we focus on one. In this case we focus on the large groups as an appropriate area in which to communicate God's saving and liberating word. The exercises in this section assume that people rarely think, much less act, in large-group categories. They attempt to help people begin to do that on all four levels of learning: affective, cognitive, active, and votive.

This theoretical explanation is meant for the background reading of the enabler and for those interested in the cognitive form of communication. However, it does not presume to be a definitive statement nor does it assume that cognitive theory is enough to move people to social change. A whole new perception involving feeling, commitments, and actions must be added to the theory. As the Bible says, it is necessary to love God, not only with one's mind, but with one's heart, soul, and strength . . . all of them.

3. FOUR TYPES OF POWER

In our discussion of how a large group functions, "power to change" is identified as an important dimension in solving large-group problems. The following is an attempt to clarify what we mean by power and to consider what kinds of power are appropriate or inappropriate for use by church groups.

The greatest uproar and confusion in churches in the last few decades has centered around the church and politics. Some believe the church should have nothing to do with politics; others believe politics is central to the church's mission. The uproar between these folks, it seems, is based in great part on the confusing of four different kinds of power. An effort to distinguish them can go a long way to settling the uproar and will probably help gain support for the appropriate use of power by churches if it is properly defined.

The activist sees nonactivists as moralistic purists who are not willing to mix their religion and politics, or even as mossbacks whose protests against mixing religion and politics are really efforts to support the status quo. The nonactivist sees activists as consumed with ambition for power and captured by the style, language and tactics of power politics, which is contrary to simple, humble Christian life. The unfortunate standoff between these camps results from an exaggeration of both positions.

There is truth and error in both these exaggerations. The nonactivist rightly fears what we will call *power politics.* The activist correctly fears the naive, ineffective innocence we will call *moralistic power.* But between these two exaggerated positions are two other types of power use that are appropriate for churches to employ, teach, recommend, and support. We will call them *moral power* and *political power.* Let us clarify these distinctions.

1. *Moralistic power* is very personal but it has social consequences. Its followers have the answers for everyone; we can stop looking. Its goal is to see that society as a whole follows a particular personal moral code. If it did, stability and order would prevail. In order to encourage this, the benefits of this social order should go first to those who most perfectly follow the code. When change in society occurs, it should result in advantages to the deserving, who can more wisely decide social policy and rules for social inter-

course. The use of force is seen as necessary sometimes but only against enemies with evil intent. The Bible is often referred to in a selected way for support, especially passages about how God blesses the righteous with prosperity. The church's role is, therefore, to uplift the righteous, to build the moral fiber, to pray for and support all in authority.

Tactics of moralistic power vary from the complete rejection of all public concerns in favor of a personal mysticism to the active use of public power in organizations, in media, and on the outskirts of government (e.g., certain kinds of chaplaincies), while denying that one is using this power by means of clothing it in religious language. One subtle tactic in the use of moralistic power is the act of "dangerous innocence." This is an expression of genuine personal care for some one person, the consequences of which are very harmful to others. A small example: while you are driving in traffic, the car in front of you "generously" stops to let one car make a left turn in front of your line of traffic. This holds up two or more persons while letting one proceed. This generous act results in a benefit to one person and a delay for two or more. This "dangerous innocence" is unfortunately a popular view of what people mean when they say, "That's a Christian thing to do."

2. *Moral power* is very different from moralistic power. Its goal is global well-being for all people and nature, for each aspect of people and nature is interlocked in an ecological and spiritual web. The exercise of power should benefit the have-nots. Social change should result in a redistribution of resources and decision-making power to all. On any given issue, decisions should be made by those most affected by the issue. Violence is not used, because it is a means that violates the ends it seeks. People are themselves ends, not means. Nonviolent means are thus perfected to provide necessary defense for persons and society. The expected results are long-term. Moral power sees this approach to be the same as Jesus' militant nonviolence. Thus, the church's role is to redistribute political, economic, and social power without gaining this power for itself.

In doing this, the church encourages activities that are within the political system but also some which are outside the normal political processes, such as protests, attempts at persuasions, noncooperation, and intervention. These latter actions are the general categories that Gene Sharp uses,* under which he lists almost 200 practical nonviolent tactics (see Supportive Resources for this list). Most of these, like sit-ins and boycotts, are outside the structure of party politics and are often called "direct action." They are especially useful to the exercise of moral power because they are often the only means available to oppressed groups. In addition, these tactics can be applied where normal political power is relatively ineffective— namely, on economic issues. If a company does not pay a living wage as determined by the workers, then a strike by workers rather than a vote for a congressional representative may do the job.

Finally, moral power is gained and used in a much different way from other power. It appeals more to people's sense of fair play than to their votes. The moral credit a person or group builds up depends on the perceived "rightness" of their cause rather than the money or political power they amass. Trust is very high. Noble and courageous acts are expected. Moral power can win even when it apparently loses, as when it invokes overreaction from a political power, exposing it to be power politics—for example, the creation of martyrs. Brute force undermines political power because political power finally rests on the trust and credibility of moral power.

3. What then is *political power?* This is power of the duly ordained representatives and their appointees. All people are more or less represented in theory in a given political territory. The goal of political power is the welfare and order within that territory and the protection of those borders. So, of course, the benefits of this political power go only to those people within the boundaries. All people outside are seen as adversaries or as allies against other adversaries. Political power is gained by politicians for themselves, with the understanding that this power is then to be used for the benefit of others. The decisions are made in theory by representatives for all the people. No criteria of the "most affected" or the "most righteous" are applied. Violence is used, but only by the state, as legal, controlled violence. The results of the exercise of political power are immediate and short-term. The Bible is frequently referred to in

The Politics of Nonviolent Action (Boston: Porter Sargent, 1973).

support of representative use of power. Church and state are separate in principle but cooperative when sectarianism is avoided. The church encourages active participation in this political process. Tactics for working in the political power system include registering voters, poll watching, voting, lobbying, political party work, petition signing, referenda, letter writing, visitations, and petitioning for the redress of grievances.

Each of these activities has many subtle aspects requiring special skills for effectiveness which churches can justifiably teach without losing their integrity or independence as a church. The line for church involvement in politics has to be drawn, however, when political power becomes power politics.

4. *Power politics* requires even greater skill because it is a highly developed art. Its goals are not a better world. Its entire purpose is to gain power as an end in itself. The benefactors are those who have power, and "to them more will be given." Politicians gain and exercise power for themselves and their immediate supporters, although many pious pledges and patronage payments are made to others. The decisions are, of course, reserved for the winners. To the victors belong the spoils. Violence is used wherever necessary to maintain those in power. The results are immediate and important only during the reign of those exercising power or their appointed heirs.

The Bible is rarely referred to and morality is placed in the moralistic box and as such is seen as irrelevant to the real exercise of power. The church, however, is used occasionally to bless those in power if it is kept on a personal and/or abstract plane. Occasionally, churches themselves get into using power politics. Classically it's called "the church triumphant and militant" or "theology of glory." Today, this activity is an overreaction to moralistic power and is rightly criticized by those who want to keep the church out of power politics.

The specific tactics of power politics have given it a bad name, but these tactics are essential for us to understand. They are directly tied to the assumptions and realities of a dominant/dependent social structure. As such, all social control mechanisms are called in for use in power politics. These will be discussed in the section on the use of power.

The following chart helps us to see the four types of power graphically:

Chart of Four Types of Power

Type	Moralistic Power	Moral Power	Political Power	Power Politics
1. Goal	Observance of personal moral code	Global justice	General welfare of one nation	Power itself
2. Who benefits	The righteous	Have-nots first, then haves	Political constituency	The haves
3. Who makes decisions	Those in authority	Those most affected	Representative spokespeople	The strongest
4. Use of violence	Only against evil	None	Only legal violence	No restraint when maintenance of power is at stake
5. When results are expected	Immediate	Long-term	Immediate and short-term	Immediate
6. Bible use	Selectively used	Jesus' militant, nonviolent redistribution of power	Used to support representative government; cooperative when nonsectarian	Considered irrelevant
7. Tactics used	Mystical escape or politics in religious clothing, or dangerous innocence	Protest, persuasion, non-cooperation, intervention	Exercise of constitutional rights	Use of social-control mechanisms

Base of church
identity and
constant action

Realm of
limited church
activity when
possible

Only areas of appropriate
church use of power

II. ENVISIONING ALTERNATIVES

OVERVIEW

Envisioning is an important aspect of working for social change. It goes beyond problem solving by looking toward what might and can be. A vision of the future gives a perspective from which to evaluate the present and acts as a guide for social change efforts.

The first envisioning exercise, Visioning the Good World, is a priority building exercise. It is important to help people personally and corporately to construct their own visions of the kingdom as it is informed by the biblical vision. Many examples of visions from the Bible are offered in the supplementary resources. (Note the social dimensions of these visions.) Therefore, these exercises could easily be lengthened to a three-hour session or to two sessions if people are asked to study and meditate on these visions to help shape their own. Allow as much time as you can for people to dream and envision. You may choose to use the Visionaries' Checklist here rather than in the exercise We Have Rights.

Every vision of a future good world implies some grievance about the present world. Visioning Independence is an exercise to help people clarify, act out, and reflect on a list of grievances guided by the original Declaration of Independence and a modern economic version of it.

Both Needs, Wants, Haves and Needs and Frills are two exercises that help people sort out and commit themselves to a new, simple life-style that is conscious of the burdens of affluence. Duplication of work sheets is helpful so each individual can have one on which to work.

The two exercises on rights help people to determine for themselves, and together, the role of government in their ideal world, its needed benefits and necessary constraints. The questionnaire is needed to test how much people really do support the concepts of the Bill of Rights with the use of different language. They Have Rights moves people to action by the actual exercise of the right of petitioning government for the redress of grievances. Many people have never done this kind of letter writing before. Even if they have, there are never too many letters from citizens to Representatives. The actual experience is very important for people to have. Encourage people to organize their own daily lives so that correspondence with their elected officials becomes a regular experience.

The readings that accompany these exercises on envisioning provide a firm theological foundation. In order to project a more desirable future and one closer to what we understand God's intentions to be, it is important that we read, reflect and dialogue on God's historic and ever present words and action. These readings shed light not only on the envisioning exercises but on our efforts in religious commitment to social change.

EXERCISES IN ENVISIONING ALTERNATIVES

VISIONING THE GOOD WORLD   **PART 1 AWARENESS/ANALYSIS**

PURPOSE:
To encourage hope in a better future and to provide a process for envisioning that future.

ASSUMPTIONS:
Social change assumes a vision of a better world toward which one seeks change.

Constant awareness of that vision is essential to its achievement.

Learning how to discern what we want the world to be is a difficult skill, but it is a skill that can be acquired.

PREPARATION:
People probably will find deliberate dreaming hard to do until they are supported and encouraged and until they connect it with their own fantasy life. It is necessary to keep "permitting" and encouraging people to dream. Make a selection or two from the Biblical Visions List to be used during the meditation.

TIME:
1 hour or, better, extend the time, if possible, to two hours by doubling the length of each step.

MATERIALS:
Bibles
Copies of Biblical Visions List
Contemporary Visions
Declaration of Independence
Paper and pencils
Newsprint and markers

PROCEDURE:

A. Meditation: *(30 minutes)*
1. Explain the need of a vision to guide one's way. Everybody has a vision of some sort about the future. The issue is: Is that vision my own or was it given to me by mass media and advertising or by some other source?

2. Make the following proclamation: "All gathered here are hereby recognized as the community visionaries." These "visionaries" are now assigned to dream up the best of all worlds, possible or not. Ease people into meditating on a vision by asking them to:

a. Relax. Take a comfortable position. Close your eyes. Put yourself in a positive mood. Smile to yourself. Mentally remove yourself from any annoying situation you may be presently facing. (Pause between each of these directions to provide people time enough to adjust.)

b. Unleash all restraints and dream of the wildest, most perfect world possible. It does not need to be practical or even feasible.

c. Make it a worldwide vision with real people, about fifty years from now. Consider all the institutions you would include, national and international. *(3–5 minutes)*

d. Enjoy yourself in this world you have created. See your relatives and friends, those you care about enjoying this world with you. *(3 minutes)*

e. Now, let's ease back to this time and space. With your eyes still closed, become conscious of the place you are in, feel the chairs or floor that is supporting you. Think of the state and city and building. Think of the people here with you. Slowly open your eyes.

f. Jot down some of the main themes of your dream trip. Record the highlights of your vision. *(3 minutes)*

3. Listen to some of God's dreams as recorded in the Bible. (Read aloud your biblical selection. You might also read from Contemporary Visions.) Take time now to reflect and continue to expand your vision.

4. After 10 minutes have the group pair off and share their visions of the good world with each other. Identify the personal and social dimensions. Compare similarities, differences, contradictions. *(10 minutes)*

B. Biblical Comparisons: *(15 minutes)*
5. Pass out duplicated sheets of Biblical Visions to the pairs of visionaries.

6. Ask the pairs to read them to each other as they compare their visions with the Bible's. One reads as the other compares her or his vision in light of religious values, roots, and heritage.

C. Plenary Reports: *(20 minutes)*
7. Ask for volunteers to present their visions on newsprint to the group. Three will do. Take time to ask people how they felt about this experience.

8. Assignments for the next session:

a. Carry your vision with you and work on it when you think of a new idea.

b. List on the back of your vision paper other dreams, promises, rose gardens, future happiness schemes you hear of in the media or from friends, e.g., "Your Bahamas cruise awaits," "You can be beautiful if . . . ," etc. How do these relate to your vision, to the biblical vision?

c. Read the Declaration of Independence in preparation for Part 2.

9. Conclude with the challenge that if you don't have your own vision of the good world, others will foist theirs on you.

SUPPORTIVE RESOURCES:
Biblical Visions List (page 116)
Contemporary Visions (pages 116–17)
Declaration of Independence (pages 118–19)

VISIONING INDEPENDENCE PART 2 ACTION/REFLECTION

PURPOSE:
To help people apply their vision of the future to present social realities in the form of a declaration of independence.

ASSUMPTIONS:
Every vision of the future implies a declaration of independence from a set of conditions in the present.
It is helpful to use the past Declaration of Independence for insight into the present and to understand the spirit as well as the letter of the Declaration of Independence as it applies to life today and to our vision of the future.

PREPARATION:
Read over resources and be ready to make connections between the past and the present.

TIME:
1½ hours

MATERIALS:
Individual visions written down from Visioning the Good World (Part 1)
The Declaration of Independence, 1776
"On Economic Freedom," Jeremy Rifkin
Paper and pencils
Newsprint and marker

PROCEDURE:

A. Beginning Options: *(10 minutes)*
A dramatic reading of the Declaration of Independence by a person, preferably dressed as Thomas Jefferson, or read Declaration in a litany fashion, taking parts. Have someone list in summary form on newsprint the grievances against the King.

B. Work Session: *(20 minutes)*
   1. Post the members' visions (from previous exercise) in view of all.
   2. Have the group count off in twos "Self-evident . . . truths."
   3. In teams of two list your grievances. That is, write in summary form the list of present obstructions to attaining your vision.

C. Negotiation: *(15 minutes)*
   1. People should now go around the room trying to get signatures to their declaration.
   2. Negotiating changes and combining items should be encouraged.

D. Input for Refinement: *(15 minutes)*
   1. Have "Thomas Jefferson" or anyone present read aloud "On Economic Freedom" by Jeremy Rifkin. He or she should then "nail" or attach it to the "King's Door" (the wall).
   2. Allow 10 minutes for refinements of people's declarations and have the pairs select one statement to attach to the "King's Door."

E. Final Document: *(30 minutes)*
   1. A committee should summarize or combine these declarations into a single list of grievances. Join as many statements together as feasible. The final declaration should be as representative as possible.
   2. All people are asked to sign this document, which will be sent to the editor of the local newspaper as a present-day application of the Declaration of Independence. It also can be used for a Fourth of July speech. The point is to have it made public in some arena that is significant to the signers.

SUPPORTIVE RESOURCES:
Declaration of Independence, 1776 (pages 118–19)
"On Economic Freedom" by Jeremy Rifkin (pages 120–21)

NEEDS, WANTS, HAVES*   PART 1 AWARENESS/ANALYSIS

PURPOSE:
To help persons clarify, assess, and evaluate their needs, wants, and material/spiritual possessions.

ASSUMPTIONS:
One step to social consciousness is to know and to decide on what you want and distinguish it from what you need and have.

PREPARATION:
This exercise is especially useful for intergenerational groups: children, youth, and adults together. So include all groups where possible. The room needs to be arranged to aid participants in both private and group work. The first requires privacy, and chairs can simply be arranged in rows. However, the time will come when groups need to talk in circles, so portable chairs without tables may be best.

TIME:
1 hour

MATERIALS:
Copies of Needs, Wants, Haves List   Newsprint, markers
Copies of Needs, Wants, Haves Assessment Sheet   Pencils

PROCEDURE:
1. Pass out Needs, Wants, Haves List and Needs, Wants, Haves Assessment Sheet to each person. Have people quietly and privately assess needs, wants, and haves. *(15 minutes)*
2. Ask total group to make circles of six to eight persons. Take 5 minutes for people in groups to respond to each of the three areas of assessment. Small groups may consist of several families, or mix all persons at random. *(15 minutes)*
3. Next, have younger people meet in one part of room, older people in another and discuss: How did younger and older needs, wants, haves differ? How were they similar? Why? Each group should then summarize their basic needs. List these on newsprint. *(15 minutes)*
4. Reassemble and place newsprint lists of needs on wall side by side. Compare lists of younger and older groups. Encourage further discussion of questions or observations. *(15 minutes)*
5. If this group intends to do (Part 2 Action/Reflection) Needs and Frills, it is necessary to collect the assessment sheets to use in that exercise.

Needs, Wants, Haves List
According to your own definition, check the following as "needs" (N) or "wants" (W). Also check H if you think you now have what is listed:

N W H
___ ___ ___ 1. Love
___ ___ ___ 2. More than five shirts
___ ___ ___ 3. A job
___ ___ ___ 4. Fulfillment in job
___ ___ ___ 5. Underarm spray deodorant
___ ___ ___ 6. Two cars
___ ___ ___ 7. Health insurance
___ ___ ___ 8. Acceptance by other people
___ ___ ___ 9. Meat at every meal
___ ___ ___ 10. The capacity to love
___ ___ ___ 11. Time to relax
___ ___ ___ 12. Television

___ ___ ___ 13. Air conditioning
___ ___ ___ 14. Water
___ ___ ___ 15. Realization and acceptance of God's love *(I know God loves me)*
___ ___ ___ 16. More than two pairs of shoes
___ ___ ___ 17. Praise and appreciation from friends
___ ___ ___ 18. Hostess Twinkies
___ ___ ___ 19. Several close friends
___ ___ ___ 20. Haircuts
___ ___ ___ 21. Wearing current styles of wearing apparel
___ ___ ___ 22. An opportunity to cry

*Considerably adapted from "Needs, Wants, Haves," in *Metamorphosis: Christians Choosing Change for a World in Crisis* by Richard B. Poteet et al. © 1975 John Knox Press. Used by permission.

— — — 23. Alcoholic beverages
— — — 24. One close friend with unconditional love and acceptance
— — — 25. Belief that nothing can cause ultimate harm.
— — — 26. Going out to dinner once a week
— — — 27. A college education
— — — 28. Hair spray
— — — 29. Three meals a day
— — — 30. Being a part of the church
— — — 31. Housing
— — — 32. A bed
— — — 33. Candy
— — — 34. A place to scream
— — — 35. Time to be alone
— — — 36. Magazines
— — — 37. The right to a decent standard of living
— — — 38. The Bible
— — — 39. Paper plates and styrofoam cups
— — — 40. Opportunities to travel
— — — 41. Self-respect
— — — 42. Dreams

— — — 43. Geritol
— — — 44. Receiving or giving music
— — — 45. White sidewall tires
— — — 46. Coffee
— — — 47. Appreciation for nature
— — — 48. Pets
— — — 49. Alpo for pets
— — — 50. More than twenty toys
— — — 51. Sports
— — — 52. Competition
— — — 53. Physical health
— — — 54. Close family relations
— — — 55. Control over my life
— — — 56. Credit cards
— — — 57. Mortgages
— — — 58. Control over my work
— — — 59. Hot dogs
— — — 60. White bread
— — — 61. Greasy foods
— — — 62. Enough physical exercise
— — — 63. Equal rights
— — — 64. Privacy
— — — 65. (Other) _____

Needs, Wants, Haves Assessment Sheet

1. Draw a circle around all the things checked that you need and have. List them below:

2. List below all the things which you feel you need but you don't have:

3. List below those things you checked that you *want* and/or *have,* but do not *need:*

1.1 Do you feel pleased that most of your needs are met? Grateful? Surprised?

2.2 What stands in your way of having these needs met?

3.3 If you chose to eliminate these things from your life, what stands in your way?

NEEDS AND FRILLS

PART 2 ACTION/REFLECTION

PURPOSE:
To help people act out their own choices of needs and to reflect on that action.

ASSUMPTIONS:
Adequate self-understanding of needs and wants must be reflectively experienced.
Sacrifice is a religious need, and to eliminate some wants is a liberating experience.

PREPARATION:
Read about world hunger and update facts where necessary.
Duplicate World Food Crisis: Facts and Figures sheets and Frills Fast cards. Arrange chairs in two facing rows.

TIME:
1 hour

MATERIALS:
World Food Crisis: Facts and Figures sheets
Frills Fast pledge cards
Large Bible
Needs, Wants, Haves Assessment Sheets from preceding exercise

PROCEDURES:

A. Beginning: *(15 minutes)*
1. Pass out World Food Crisis sheets.
2. Ask people to read one fact each, aloud and in order, one after the other.
3. Take Needs, Wants, Haves Assessment sheets and individually rework them in light of these facts.

B. Group Work: *(15 minutes)*
1. Have people count off in twos "needs . . . wants . . . needs," etc. "Needs" people sit in one row of chairs facing "Wants" in the other row.
2. "Wants" people say to "Needs" people sitting across from them "I want . . ." and read off a want from their list.
3. "Needs" people ask "Wants" people, "Do you need it?" And then "Why?"
4. Proceed down list of "Wants" and "Needs" and then reverse "Wants" and "Needs" questioning.
5. People can adjust their individual assessment lists according to learnings from this exercise.

C. Choose a Frill: *(15 minutes)*
Ask people to look at #3 of Assessment Sheet list (what you want and/or have but do not need) and select one or all items for a Frills Fast.
Pass out pledge cards and ask people to enter their frills on the pledge if they choose to do so. It's OK if they don't. The pledge is to go without the frill(s) for one week. The pair of people who question each other become frill watchers for each other and agree to talk about it once during the week.

D. Celebrate: *(15 minutes)*
1. Tear off sections 2.2 and 3.3 of Assessment Sheet (what stands in your way?) and hold them in one hand, pledge in the other.
2. Read Matthew 6:19-34, "Treasures on earth," and Matthew 16:21-28, "Take up your cross."
3. Sing "Simple Gifts."
4. Offer people the choice to symbolically dispose of the frills list in a trash basket (placed in front) and to put the pledge in the "Great Book of Promises, the Bible" arranged for the occasion.
5. End with a prayer. A suggestion:
Let us pray. Lord, we know that you will avenge the poor, that you will do justice for the needy. Truly the just will praise your name: the upright shall live in your presence. It is the person who keeps faith forever and who is just to the oppressed who is happy in your sight. Help us to share our bread with the hungry. Through Christ our Lord. Amen.

World Food Crisis: Facts and Figures

Compiled by Douglas A. Walrath[*]

POPULATION

1. Incredible as it seems, some 25 percent of all the persons who ever lived on this planet are alive today.[1]
2. *Population Increase Rates*

Time Period	Number of Years	Population at End	Rate of Increase
Beginnings-8000 B.C.	990,000	8 million	.015 per 1,000
8000 B.C.-A.D. 1	8,000	300 million	.36 per 1,000
A.D. 1-1750	1,750	500 million	.56 per 1,000
1750-1800	50	1,000 million	4.4 per 1,000
1800-1850	50	1,300 million	5.2 per 1,000
1850-1900	50	1,700 million	5.4 per 1,000
1900-1950	50	2,500 million	7.9 per 1,000
1950-1975	25	3,900 million	17.1 per 1,000
1975-2000	25	6,400 million	19.0 per 1,000

Source: Ansley J. Coale[2]

3. *Life Expectancy*

Year	(years)
B.C.	18
A.D.1	22
1200	33
1600	33.5
1800	35
1850	40.9
1900	49.2
1946	66.7
1960	70.0

Source: Graham T. T. Molitor[3]

4. If the world population is now growing at the rate of 2 percent a year, how long will it take it to double? Thirty-five years. If India now has 570 million people and their numbers increase at 3 percent a year, how many Indians will there be in 1980? About 690 million. And how many will there be by A.D. 2000? Double the present number, nearly 1.2 billion.[4]
5. At the global level, population growth is still the dominant source of the expanding demand for food. With world population increasing at nearly 2 percent per year, merely maintaining current per capita consumption levels will require a doubling of food production in little more than a generation.[5]

FOOD CRISIS AND CONTRIBUTING FACTORS

1. Despite all the statistical data that swirl around in news media, conference documents, and elsewhere, we seem to fail to grasp the magnitude of our calamity. Humankind is facing a situation unprecedented in history. On almost all counts, we provide adequately for only about one third of the present human family. Nonetheless, we seriously believe that we are going to perform the miracle of doubling up on all fronts and produce, in the brief span of some 25 years, much *more* food, water, energy, and forest and mineral products *than previously in all of human history.*[6]

2. Projection to 1975, and assuming that food production in 1975 will equal that of 1973, the best year ever, indicates a shortfall equivalent to the amount of food required to feed 130 million people.[7]

3. The second factor limiting output is the uniquely serious situation with respect to availability of the four critical resources used in food production: land, water, energy, and fertilizer. For the first time in modern history, each is in short supply.[8]

---

[*]Used with permission of Douglas A. Walrath, April 1975.

[1]See this note and other numbered notes on pages 57–58.

4. *Water Use*

Country	Tons of Water (per capita per day)
United States	14.5
Sweden	9.7
Japan	3.5
India	2.4

Source: Graham T. T. Molitor[9]

5. Water, not land, could become the principal restraint on the world's food production. While water-to-crop ratios vary considerably, some 400–500 pounds of water are needed for each pound of dry plant produce.[10]

6. The average American diet requires 3,500 gallons of water per day per person. Even a modest East Indian diet requires 500 gallons per day.[11]

7. While global use of nitrogen fertilizer has been climbing 9 percent annually, new fertilizer production capacity has been growing at a mere 6 percent.[12]

8. Each year an estimated half of the world's critically short food supply is consumed or destroyed by insects, molds, rodents, birds, and other pests that attack foodstuffs in the fields, during shipment, and in storage.[13]

9. One billion people live on the equivalent of $4 a week each.[14]

10. When people spend about 80 percent of their income on food (as does much of humankind), a doubling in the price of wheat or rice cannot possibly be offset by increased expenditures. Instead, the price rise drives a subsistence diet below the survival level.[15]

11. Domesticated animals consume *five times* the amount of food consumed by human beings.[16]

12. The agricultural resources—land, water, fertilizer—required to support an average North American are nearly five times those of the average Indian, Nigerian, or Colombian.[17]

13. United States has 6 percent of the world's population, and we use 50 percent of the world's raw materials and 33 percent of the world's energy. The World Wildlife Fund estimates that we overeat by 30 percent and produce 100 pounds of garbage per person per year.[18]

14. Paul Erlich has pointed out that "Each American has roughly 50 times the negative impact on the earth's life-support system as the average citizen of India." The addition of 75 million Americans (current population projections for the year 2000) "from the standpoint of ever-scarcer nonrenewable resources . . . will be the equivalent to more than ten billion Nigerians or 22 billion Indonesians."!![19]

15. While the average person in poor countries consumes about 400 pounds of grain a year, the average North American is now consuming nearly a ton of grain a year, about 100 pounds of it in the form of beer and whiskey.[20]

16. Americans daily enjoy an average consumption of protein (all sources) amounting to more than 100 grams (about four ounces). In contrast, the recommended daily dietary allowance for an average man (154 pounds) is only 70 grams; for an average woman (123 pounds) it is even less—60 grams. Putting these facts together, one can conclude that per capita U.S. consumption already is approaching *double* the dietary amount required.[21]

Notes

1. Graham T. T. Molitor, "The Coming World Struggle for Food," *The Futurist,* August 1974, p. 169.

2. Ansley J. Coale, "The History of the Human Population," *Scientific American,* September 1974, pp. 41 and 43.

3. Loc. cit.

4. Tarzie Vittachi, "The Numbers Game," *The American Way,* July 1974, p. 15.

5. Lester R. Brown, "Global Food Insecurity," *The Futurist,* April 1974, p. 56.

6. George Borgstrom, "Stark Realities," *The Other Side,* No. 3, December 1974, pp. 1 and 4. Italics added.

7. Grant Cottam, "Carrying Capacity Already Exceeded," *The Other Side,* No. 3, December 1974, p. 1.

8. Lester R. Brown and Erik P. Eckholm, "Overview: The World Food Problem," *Christianity and Crisis,* Vol. 35, No. 1, February 3, 1975, p. 2.

9. Molitor, op. cit., p. 177.

10. Ibid.

11. Adam Finnerty, "Ecological Considerations," *Creative Simplicity,* Issue No. 3, October 1974, p. 10.

12. Molitor, op. cit., p. 177.

13. Jane E. Brody, "Experts for Pest Control to Increase World's Food," *The New York Times,* October 28, 1974, p. 1.

14. "The Shakertown Pledge," p. 2. Available from the Shakertown Pledge Group, 4719 Cedar Avenue, Philadelphia, Pennsylvania 19143.

15. Brown, loc. cit.

16. Molitor, op. cit., p. 170.

17. Brown, op. cit., p. 58.

18. "The Shakertown Pledge," p. 2.

19. Ibid., pp. 2 and 3.

20. James Reston, "How to MIRV a Cow," *The New York Times,* July 7, 1974, p. 22.

21. Molitor, op. cit., p. 172.

Frills Fast Pledge Card
(My Copy)

I_____ (name)
pledge to do without:

_____
_____
_____
_____
_____
_____

for one week and will check
in once with my frill watcher,
who is _____ (name)

Frills Fast Pledge Card
(My frill watcher's copy)

I_____ (name)
pledge to do without:

_____
_____
_____
_____
_____
_____

for one week and will check
in once with my frill watcher,
who is _____ (name)

Simple Gifts*

Traditional Shaker song

'Tis a gift to be sim - ple; 'tis a gift to be free; 'tis a

gift to come down where we ought to be, and

when we find our - selves in that place just right 'twill

be in the val - ley of love and de - light.

When true sim - pli - ci - ty is gained, to

bow and to bend we shall not be a - shamed to

turn, turn will be our de - light, 'till in

turn - ing, turn - ing we come round right.

WE HAVE RIGHTS

PURPOSE:
To help clarify an alternate vision of society by defining the minimum rights persons should enjoy.

ASSUMPTIONS:
People need to distinguish their wants and needs.

People need also to have a working vision of the world.

Clarifying the basic limits and responsibilities of institutions is one way of identifying the basic rights of people.

PREPARATION:
Read over both bills of rights and be able to make corrections.

TIME:
1 hour

MATERIALS:
Copies of Questionnaire on Applied Rights
Copies of Visionaries' Checklist
Copies of The Economic Bill of Rights

The Bill of Rights, 1791
Chalkboard or newsprint and markers

PROCEDURE:

A. Begin Session: *(10 minutes)*
1. Ask people to review needs, wants, haves, and vision lists.

2. Have each person make a "bare minimum needs" list. Then, in groups of three, combine lists to develop a bill of rights stating that government should not infringe upon these rights or permit other institutions in society to do so. In fact it is expected that the government would meet the needs and protect the rights.

3. Pass out Visionaries' Checklist to make sure the groups have listed all the points they want to.

B. Plenary Session: *(30 minutes)*
1. List on one side of chalkboard or large newsprint all the rights. Avoiding broad categories, be as specific as possible. Leave room for second parallel listing.

2. Then ask people to brainstorm all the groups of people who are without these rights. Circle names of groups of people who are in *greatest* need of these rights. As each right is called out, people can come forward and write in the names of these groups parallel to the rights listed already. This list can be titled They Have Rights.

3. Pass out samples of the Economic Bill of Rights to people to compare with their own and refine.

C. Assignments:
Before next session:

1. One half of the group might take the Economic Bill of Rights or their own bill of rights and interview two people each to test if they agree, disagree, or don't know.

2. Other half can take the Questionnaire on Applied Rights and test it on two people each.

SUPPORTIVE RESOURCES:
Questionnaire on Applied Rights (page 123)
Visionaries' Checklist (page 124)
The Economic Bill of Rights (page 125)
The Bill of Rights, 1791 (page 126)

THEY HAVE RIGHTS PART 2 ACTION/REFLECTION

PURPOSE:
To become aware of people who are without the rights that we affirm.

ASSUMPTIONS:
A workable vision including the rights of people should also contain some restraints upon the government. Surveys have shown that a majority of people don't yet believe in the Bill of Rights adopted in 1791, and yet our task today is to build upon them even greater rights to provide for an interdependent world.

PREPARATION:
Obtain names of your Representatives and Senators. Copies of their voting records would be helpful.

TIME:
1 hour

MATERIALS:
Copies of Writing an Effective Letter
Writing paper, stamps, envelopes
Copies of Forms of Address for Government Officials

PROCEDURE:

A. Beginning: *(10 minutes)*
    1. Report in and tabulate surveys on the Economic Bill of Rights and the Questionnaire on Applied Rights. Ask what we learn from these surveys.
    2. Ask people to select one area and one group of people in need that they are most aware of and take that one area as their project for action. Remind people that all of this awareness and information is useless unless they do something.
    3. Pass out Writing an Effective Letter and Forms of Address for Government Officials.

B. Work Session: *(30 minutes)*
    1. Ask people to write a letter to their Representative, individually.
    2. The letter can express a general concern if people do not know specific legislation. They can simply ask the legislator for information, hearing reports, etc. It is important that people actually write the letter, then and there, and send it.
    3. Offer to help write the letter and to correct it or improve it.

C. Concluding Session: *(20 minutes)*
    1. As letters are completed, stamped, and addressed, each person should be ready to mail the letter.
    2. The group might join in singing and sharing prayers (suggestion: "This Little Light of Mine").
    3. Then walk to the mailbox, singing or quietly meditating on the way.

SUPPORTIVE RESOURCES:
Writing an Effective Letter (page 127)
Correct Forms of Address for U.S. Government Officials (page 127)
Forms of Address for Canadian Government Officials (page 128)

BACKGROUND READINGS ON ENVISIONING ALTERNATIVES

1. RELIGIOUS VISIONS

The exercises in Grasping the Social Conditions sought to build consciousness of the social, large-group dimensions of life as the first step in social change. The second step is an active awareness of alternatives to the social conditions in which people are caught. Thinking about alternatives takes many forms: fantasy, dreams, visions, hopes, expectations, blueprints, plans, schemes of all sorts. The land of milk and honey, the hope for a better life, the shalom world, the peaceable kingdom, the kingdom of God are all examples of alternatives to our current conditions. Such visions are natural and essential to social change. They are dangerous when we get carried away by them, for they can mislead the dreamer to flights of fancy that are hopeless dead ends and perhaps even dangerous escapes from reality. However, we are short on the vision side and long on the reality side in our "can do," pragmatic, industrial society. We North Americans are doers, and we hold little honor for visionaries and dreamers, which unfortunately leaves all the apostles, saints, and martyrs on the sidelines. This imbalance needs correction in our education for social change, because without vision and clear alternatives we don't know what we are doing, we don't know what we stand for, and we don't know where the change we seek is going to end. Without a clearly stated and affirmed vision, we are often manipulated to react against, or blindly support, the prevailing rules and structures. A vision is essential, especially in the darkest days of a struggle.

A vision does a number of things for us: (1) It gives us staying power, (2) It keeps us ready to act when the time is right, (3) It motivates planning, (4) It unites people, (5) It is a positive, spiritually affirming activity, and (6) It is a self-transcending religious act. A vision carries us through the long haul on the way to the promised land. A vision can be a mere mirage in the wasteland, but we will never get out of the wasteland unless we have a picture of the future to guide us.

1. Recently, a church group visited some congressional staff people who were working on tax reform in the U.S. House of Representatives. The staff members gave complex explanations of parts of a tax reform bill. They reported that they had just written a 500-page book explaining another 700 pages of a very watered-down tax reform bill which, after a year and a half of work, would not be likely to pass the Senate, but if it did, the President would probably veto it. Then someone asked a personal question of one staff person: "Doesn't that make you question your whole vocational choice?" He said, "No, because if we were not doing all of this, we would not be ready when the time comes for *real* tax reform." This man had a vision that seemed spiritually to carry him through the wasteland of defeated legislation. *Visions provide staying power.*

2. Envisioning alternatives is a part of getting ready. Indeed, we often experience a very active fantasy life when we are denied the things we want. Sometimes when our intentions are frustrated, we give up in despair. A better approach, however, is to use defeat as a welcome period of reflection, evaluation, and a time to ask ourself and our group, What do we *really* want? What would we do if there were no obstacles? Do you know what you would do if you won a lottery? In a rapidly changing world, we can never predict when our chance will come. Even the fool who is ready will find the doors opened when it's least expected. Jesus taught this need for readiness in several parables such as the wise and foolish virgins (Matthew 25:1-3) and the rich fool (Luke 12:13-21). *Visions keep us ready to act.*

3. The worse a social condition becomes, the easier it is to envision alternatives. It motivates the planning of alternative worlds. Planning our ideal world is a part of the genius of inspired people. Moses and Aaron did it in the wilderness. Jesus often spoke of the kingdom. Augustine wrote about the Cities of God and Man. Immanuel Kant wrote about a United Nations in the eighteenth century. Gandhi and Nehru envisioned an independent India, even while in British jails. Envisioning is a strange human ability that requires the highest forms of imagination and daydreaming combined with a hard discipline of schematizing all kinds of possible consequences and alternative scenarios. *Visions motivate planning.*

4. A clear vision that is shared by a group forms a very powerful cohesive bond in that group, and this unity is necessary for a group to accomplish its goals. The promise of milk and honey united the children of Israel. Martin Luther King's dreams of

an integrated society united Blacks in the United States. The common vision of national independence has welded together colonies all over the world from the American colonies in the 1700s to the African nations in the 1900s. *A vision unites people.*

5. Envisioning is positive thinking that energizes people. Constant negative protest will deplete energy. Vietnam stimulated the resurgence of the anti-war movement. It took several years and the wisdom of older pacifists to encourage the change of emphasis from "against war" to "for peace." It was necessary to begin to look at the possibilities of a world at peace and to work for those changes that would not only eliminate what was evil but, more importantly, to begin to create better alternatives. *Visions are positive and spiritually affirming.*

6. The ability to envision must be developed if there is to be any hope for social change. Envisioning is the preliminary step before a group sets its goals in a planning process. Visioning is not like hindsight thinking. We know how wise we can be in hindsight. We see, after it is all over, what we *should* have done. Visioning is an attempt to see all this *before* it's over. Visioning is *foresight* thinking and planning. It is hindsight backwards. It requires the ability to ignore, at least for a while, all practical, measurable results. One must be immune to those put-down words, "Be realistic." People in education for social change need to say in response what one rarely hears: "Be idealistic." "Be a visionary," at least for a while.

Most of all, envisioning requires hope. "Faith," we are told in Hebrews 11:1, "is the assurance of things hoped for, the conviction of things not seen." Indeed, hope is the central spiritual category that holds large groups together. Hope is always future looking. Thus it is not protective of the status quo. *Envisioning is a self-transcending act.*

What is most critical for Christians, however, is *what,* besides the status quo, they hope for. Let's back off and see where we get our dreams and visions. Some dreams are actually nightmares. Some visions are like Hitler's *Mein Kampf.* What makes the difference between a good and a bad vision of the future?

For the Christian it could be said that finally, a vision must be inspired by God to be a good vision. But what does "inspired by God" mean in everyday language and how do you get such inspiration? The answer requires a careful statement of what we mean by the word God and a few other basic theological concepts. So there follows a theological survival kit intended for lightweight traveling. The person who has little time for profound theological reflection needs nevertheless a few basic staples of meaning for nourishment through the spiritual wastelands. This kit is meant to be torn out and stuffed in your briefcase, knapsack or diary, or wherever you put important documents for your journey.

2. A THEOLOGICAL SURVIVAL KIT

For the people who are committed to follow Jesus in the Christian life, there is a vision of a new city, of God's shalom (the meaning of Jerusalem). It is a new city or human community where God dwells with people and where "he will wipe away every tear from their eyes, and death shall be no more [Rev. 21:4]." In this vision, the hungry are fed, the strangers are welcomed, the naked are clothed, the sick and imprisoned are cared for. (See Matthew 25:31-46.)

Biblical visions are visions of a social structure, a community of love, peace, and fairness. But, strangely, these visions have been reduced in recent times from the public community to the private, personal sphere of our consciousness. So when we begin to daydream about the future, it very often is a private or family affair—something like an ideal Christmas day—rather than a vision of a land of peace and justice. Our visions keep getting reduced to shopping centers full of more consumer goods and more wonders of technological wizardry.

Upon reflection we do expand our hopes and dreams to include spiritual qualities of love and affection. But here the hope usually still remains *private* and without redeeming *social* value.

Part of the problem is simply in the words we use and the way we use them. As in the background readings for the first section, where we translated and charted some theological terms beyond their psychological meanings to their social meanings, we will now expand this translation to include nine key theological terms. There are many more, of course, and we will only graze the surface meanings of these terms. But these nine terms are probably the most essential for a basic understanding of Christian theology. They are like the essential features of, say, driving a car: steering wheel, brake, gas pedal. There is infinitely more to a car—and to theology—but we can learn as we drive and call on technicians for details. Here we will continue to translate the meanings from the private perspective to the small-group (interpersonal) and large-group (intergroup) perspective. We continue to assume: (1) that all three levels are important, (2) that the Bible did not limit these terms to the private world as we tend to, and (3) that the rich wisdom of our basic Christian teaching is enough to inspire us, if we can free it from the limitations of a solely private perspective.

The following kit contains the essential meaning that we need in order to survive in a world full of nightmares and corrupting dreams that bind us to dependence.

The major themes in this theological survival kit are:

1. God
2. Jesus Christ
3. Holy Spirit
4. Cross
5. Resurrection
6. Sin
7. Repentance
8. Salvation
9. Morality

1. God as the Power of Mystery

One of the many traits religious people have assigned to God through the ages is power. God is almighty, all powerful, omnipotent. This is only one trait we have given God among such other traits as loving, all knowing, just, gracious, merciful. But for the purposes of this book, the attribute of God's power is central. It is the driving force in the process of large-group relationships. We can understand power as the effect of divine mystery.

What do we mean when we say God is all powerful? Like all anthropomorphic or human attributions to the divine, "power" is a human word that reflects the limitations of people who are locked in time and space—unable to understand, much less fully describe, God. The Eastern church understood this human limitation and very early said that all human concepts of gods were idols. We can appreciate this mystery on an interpersonal level. We can never fully name or describe even a close personal friend without missing many subtle aspects of that person. As the poet John Ciardi says, "If I could understand my wife, I would forget to go home." The relationship remains only if the mystery continues.

Not only are we incapable of fully defining another person, but even to try to do so is a little insulting, because it makes that person into a very forgettable object of one's limiting concepts, mental pictures, or abstractions. One proud grandmother responded to a compliment about her grandson, "Oh! You should see his pictures!"

Just as our concepts tend to become idols or abstractions that dehumanize people, our descriptions of God often help us dismiss God and settle for our controllable mental pictures of God. The common ingredient in the respectful treatment of our friends and our God is the need to give up our efforts of completely defining and thus limiting them. There is a mystery about our closest friends and relatives. But God is the ultimate mystery and far beyond any of our definitions. Thomas Aquinas said, "He knows God best who acknowledges that whatever he thinks and says falls short of what God really is." (*In librum De causis, lectio* 6).

We do not, however, just stop talking about our friends and about God just because they are finally mysterious. Indeed, if we look at mystery in our lives, which means to study the effects this mystery has, then we discover some amazing things. Thomas Aquinas said, "We can demonstrate the existence of God from His effects; though from them we cannot know God perfectly as he is in His essence." (*Summa Theologica,* Part 1, Question 11, Article 3).

Have you ever used the power of a mysterious box on children? If you bring a box with wrapping paper and a ribbon on it into a room of children and tell them they should not open it, you will observe some strange behavior. Nothing else will capture their attention but the box, its imagined contents, and schemes for getting it open. The same phenomenon is true for adults in every aspect of life. Mystery is extremely powerful. Mystery drives people to incredible feats of endurance: to reach mountaintops, to win the love of a lover, or to unravel a scientific mystery. One missing piece in a jigsaw puzzle will send a family household into a frenzy. Mystery is extremely powerful.

Rudolph Otto wrote about this phenomenon in *The Idea of the Holy.* He pointed out how the concept of "the Holy" both attracts and repels us. He spoke of God as the fascinating and terrifying mystery. God cannot be defined, but we can study God's aspects and the effects they have on people. The most powerful aspect of God is God's mystery. The most powerful aspect of all life is mystery. And the most powerful motivating force in people is the complex moments of attraction and terror toward mystery. Fear of unknown things and desire for other unknown things are two strings that pull us through our emotional and spiritual lives.

Now when we say God is almighty and all powerful, we are saying that there is a reality that moves and causes other things to move by means of an unknowable and mysterious process. This mystery is its own determination. "God has his own will" is the way theologians used to say it. We mean by this that, at least, "I don't understand it, but I certainly acknowledge its reality and its effects." God is mystery, and this mystery motivates life. It is terrifying in that I have no control over it and that it is capable of destroying me. But it is ultimately attractive, because I am irresistibly drawn to it, like an all powerful-magnet. "I cannot rest," as Augustine said, "until I find rest in thee." God is mystery. In this God is all powerful.

Now let us compare this view to the views that tend to be held in the more traditional, individualized religion and in the modern small-group or interpersonal perspective. Rather than focusing on God as a power in history, the ruler over nations, individualized religion tends to see God as father,* a family deity and authority who judges and disciplines his children. God is aware of every hair on my head as he is each bird in the air. Like a father, God provides my daily bread and forgives my debts. God is my patron. I am God's prodigal (or elder) son or daughter. As for a lost sheep, my shepherd God will leave the flock to bring me back and call out the angelic chorus to celebrate my return. There are no pictures here of God delivering a whole nation of people out of slavery in Egypt. The only exodus is out of my private slavery to alcoholism, despair, or grief. This is not an inaccurate perspective. But it is only part of the picture.

The small-group or interpersonal perspective focuses on God as love. God pulls together brothers and sisters in the family. God unites two estranged friends or lovers. Some religiously oriented small-group leaders hinge their theological ideas on the phrase "God is love, therefore love is God!" If you feel love, that is God. This is the beginning of religious understanding for many people, because it does express a basic human experience, love, which almost everybody has. And love is a spiritual reality that cannot be confined to human manipulation. However, the love experience—which certainly can be of divine

*Though I do not intend to limit the qualities of God to the paternal, this has been the most common usage in traditional privatized religion.

origin—is not all of God. One cannot accurately say "love is God" because God is much more. Indeed, the biblical perspective of God points to aspects of God that we simply cannot understand. When we try to limit God to a symbol or experience like father or love, God "turns his back." Theologians call this "deus absconditus." God vanishes from us.

Although some aspects, footprints, or effects of God are like a father's judgments, love, or power, God is finally a mystery to us. We cannot ignore the private, small group, or larger-group activity of God. But God is also a god of nature and history whose mysterious presence, and *absence,* causes historical things to happen. God is not simply my private deity to whom I pray. God is the God of a *people,* a large group, a community. God is the source of shalom, the vision of a peaceful and just community of people and of just and peaceful relationship among the peoples of the world. God is also manifest in Christ and the Holy Spirit. Now let us put this in everyday language. Here is a graphic statement of the comparative views of God:

Theological Term	Individual	Interpersonal	Intergroup
God	Father	Love	Power

2. Jesus as "The Least of These"

"Do you accept Jesus as your *personal* Savior?" is the question of mass media evangelists and the question many churches ask of new members as a test of their commitment. In Sunday school we used to sing, "Jesus loves me; this I know, for the Bible tells me so." To say the Lord is *my* personal savior who loves *me* is not a problem unless you stop there. It's not untrue, it's just not the entire truth. Religion is certainly a private matter. It is deeply personal. Jesus is a person whose life, words, and deeds are to be followed, and imitated and taken very personally. That is indeed the church's teaching. But it is only part of that teaching. Jesus also is to be understood as an influence within small groups and among large groups.

In small prayer groups and sensitivity groups, warm human relationships often develop. Masks are removed and trust among people grows. A beautiful sense of love develops, so that the spirit of Jesus is "in our midst." The trusting and understanding community becomes a medium of God's love as revealed in Jesus.

No one can, with any sense of fairness, criticize this experience and the necessity of a small, trusting community for human development. But there is much more to the imitation of Jesus than the knowledge that "he loves *me*" and that he is "in our midst."

In addition to these experiences of Jesus is a view of Jesus expressed in Matthew 25. Here, Jesus identifies himself with the "least of these"—namely, the hungry, sick, naked, imprisoned, the oppressed of the world. These are large groups of people, not an individual or a family or a prayer group. Those who are hungry in our day make up a group of about 500 million people. Jesus says, "As you did it to one of the least of these my brethren, you did it to me [Matt. 25:40]."

Liberation theology simply says Jesus Christ *is* the oppressed of the world, God's elect. In Matthew 19:16-26, the rich man seeking his personal salvation is not left out, but it is harder for him to enter the kingdom than it is for a camel to go through the needle's eye. In this passage, Jesus confronts the rich man, who can't find his salvation in any of his private religious observances, with the option to sell all he has and give it to the poor—in other words, he should use his wealth for a social program for *his own* religious benefit. Jesus never excludes private religious practices but if it stops there it is hypocrisy, a tithing "of mint and dill and cumin" and a neglect of the "weightier matters of the law, justice and mercy and faith [Matt. 23:23]." These are large-group or intergroup aspects of religious practice. "These you ought to have done, without neglecting the others." Those who limit religion to their personal salvation are blind guides, "straining out a gnat and swallowing a camel [Matt. 23:23-24]." Jesus is our personal liberator, the uniter in our midst, but also the least, the oppressed of the world.

Theological Term	Individual	Interpersonal	Intergroup
Jesus	My savior who loves me	Our savior in our midst	The least of these

3. Holy Spirit as Power from Within

When the mystery of God reveals itself to us, it is terrifying. The terror of the void, of the infinities of space and time, fills us with fear. To know that we had no say in our birth and little to say in our death and that it will soon all be over for us is a painful revelation, until we begin to see that life runs on the wonder and awe of this mystery, that it is only our arrogance that makes us want to control all aspects of our life and death, space and time. It is terrifying to us only when we are comfortable in our hand-made worlds, which we assume to be absolute. We are fearful only when we trust other things than God and become anxious that we will lose them.

The wonder and awe of the mystery of life—in a flower, a sunset, a person, a starry night, or whatever checks our urge to control and sets us back in gratitude and respect—is to be enjoyed always. But the wonder at mystery is present not only *beyond* us as the "wholly other," the mystery is *within us* also. It is a rare person who always has himself or herself fully under control. If such people exist, they are terrible bores, without spontaneity, without any uncalculated responses. They have no laughter, no tears. All people have a depth of unknowing within them, which is the source of wonder and awe and self-esteem as well as the source of terror. When we are filled with self-esteem and self-respect, we marvel at ourselves and, as the Bible says, we are "full of the Holy Spirit." If that uncontrollable spirit is one of fear, anger, or hatred, then we are possessed by a demon, to use ancient language.

The Holy Spirit is a mystery within us that lifts us up and boosts our spirits. But if our self-esteem turns into arrogance, then the mystery beyond us becomes terrifying and sets us back in place. When our spirits are high, the outside world is full of wonder; it is full of things to be explored and enjoyed. When spirits are low, the opposite is true. All the world is dark and menacing to us, ready to do us in. It is reasonable to assume that these inner spirits are the same spirits to which the biblical writers were referring in their world of devils and angels. In biblical times, science had not yet drained the spirit forces from nature. There used to be a whole set of now almost archaic words to describe the way the mystical spirit worked within people.

People are "inspirited" by the Holy Spirit. Thus inspired, they can "aspire" to great things, be moved to celebrate in song and dance. If they overdo their "aspirations," trying to be more than they can be and to do more than they can do, then they fall down into hopelessness; they are "dispirited." They feel that they have lost the spirit. But a strange thing usually happens. The spirit rises again. They are "inspired" over and over until the day they "expire" in death. Death for the Bible is the final loss of the breath (literally the wind; in Hebrew, *ruach,* and in Greek, *pneuma)* of the person and of the Spirit of God.

We do not use these words derived from spirit so much today because we modern people have lost the sense of the spirit. But we use other words, such as "pressure" and "tension," to talk about these nonphysical forces that move us. Thus when we are "depressed," we may become "impressed" with something beyond us. This moves us to "express" ourselves in words and acts. If we overdo our self-expression, we become "oppressive" or "suppressive" of others and are "impressed" again by our limits and the need to "repress" ourselves.

We don't say that we need more inspiration. We say we are "under tension." We need to clarify our "intention" to "extend" ourselves, but not so far as to become "pretentious."

These are not simply word games. They are ways we have developed to talk about experiences the Bible referred to as spiritual. Words change, the experiences don't.

On a personal level, then, the Holy Spirit is the inner mystery or spirit that lifts our spirits because we hold in esteem only what we do not fully control, even ourselves. But when we are in touch with this inner mystery and in touch with the outer mystery or God as the wholly other, we are delivered from our sloth and despair on the one hand, and our arrogance and pride on the other. This deliverance is the spiritual meeting of God and people, the Christ-event. When this happens we are on a "sober high" in which we are neither in control nor out of control; we are in a kind of transcendent state where we are inspired beyond our normal capacities, yet fully aware of all that we are doing. We are in our best form, in tune with things and running smoothly. These experiences are high points that guide us through the dark valleys of our lives.

On an interpersonal level, we experience times when our spirits are in tune with others. This is sometimes called "good vibrations." It is not something we can make happen, although we do have veto power over it. The Holy Spirit is that inner mystery which urges us out of ourselves to unity with others because we are attracted by a respect and esteem for the mystery in them.

On a large-group level, the Holy Spirit interacts with the group spirit that rises to empower the whole group. The spirit of the group is the harmony of voices and actions that is beyond the power of any one individual to produce. Many times a spirit will unite a group, but it is a spirit of fear or hatred, as in a group of attacking soldiers. These spirits or demons have great power. However, instead of empowering as the Holy Spirit does, they overpower, not for the sake of God or God's attributes of truth, goodness, power, mystery, but for the sake of greed, conquest, chauvinism, etc. The Holy Spirit does not *overpower,* but *empowers* a people with God's mystery, which makes them ends not means. People are valuable for their uniqueness, their unique cultures and histories. We mean by "uniqueness" that people will not fit into our categories or abstract ideas. They are finally a mystery, an unexplainable end to be respected for no other reason than that they exist as unique beings. This is another way of saying they reflect something of the divine within them. They are made in the image of God.

As such, all persons have rights and are due respect. This is the religious reason for our social action. This is why we follow Jesus, because he spent his life lifting up those who had lost their spirit. Jesus' inner spirit was so in tune with the wonder of God's mystery in the world and in others that we say that in him God and people come together. Jesus is the Messiah, the Christ, the union of God and people.

God is the mystery of all life and the power of being. God is manifest in persons as the mystery within, or the Holy Spirit. As these aspects of reality unite the human and divine, there is the event of Christ. Jesus lived out his life, according to the Bible, by letting no demonic spirits possess him. He was overpowered by nothing, even when threatened with death. And in death he was empowered by his spirit within to forgiveness and love for others, especially the "least."

Theological Term	Individual	Interpersonal	Intergroup
Holy Spirit	Mystery within	Group harmony and spirit	Group empowering and directing

4. and 5. Crucifixion and Resurrection: The Slaughter and Uprising of the Innocent

Private religion sees the cross as Jesus suffering for *me,* so that I may, with him, overcome death. As we die with him "we are raised to eternal life," reads the funeral liturgy.

Private religion makes the cross of Jesus a high symbol on its altars, referring to death in general and to *my* personal death in particular. The cross is empty in Protestant churches as a symbol of Jesus' resurrection. Death in general is overcome, I am personally protected, as are my believing loved ones (to whom I dedicate the altar flowers), from the meaningless, empty void of death and hell. Private religion sees the resurrection as a personal conquest of death by Jesus, God's gift of God's Son for me, so I would no longer suffer the "sting of death."

Small-group religion sees the cross and resurrection as a symbolic death of our phony masked selves and a resurrection to truth and openness toward other people. The spirit of Jesus is raised in our midst if we open ourselves to trusting relationships. The fearful old Adam and Eve are crucified, and the new man and woman are resurrected to loving community.

But what about the 10,000 people or so, most of them children, who die each day of starvation and malnutrition? This question haunts us. It will not go away. These deaths are not understood by the private and interpersonal views of the cross and resurrection. Rather, it takes a larger view to begin to make sense of (not to say justify) innocent suffering and death. However helpful private and interpersonal religion may be, they do not account for the fact that these innocent deaths, like Jesus', are caused by people. Jesus' death was not just a symbol of death in the abstract or a symbol of my death, nor was it merely the death of my old, sinful self. Jesus' death on the cross is not death in general. It is murder in particular. He was killed by the religious and political power structures of his day, just as the starving people today are victims of economic and political decisions. Economic and political decisions are made by people. They are not fated abstractions in some symbolic world; they are decisions someone made, which means they did not have to be made, they were not predetermined or necessary. People are responsible and accountable for death, whether caused by violent aggression or by neglect.

The cross as seen from a social perspective is an act of historical rather than a natural given power. Rubem Alves, a liberation theologian, said, "Christ was killed as a subversive, condemned as a criminal, as a threat to the order of society, by the powers that represented the highest in law and political order, on the one hand, and law and piety on the other."*

Understood in this way, the resurrection is not merely my private gift of insurance against death. Jesus' resurrection is private, to be sure, but it is also profoundly public in that the least of these, the suffering innocent, start an uprising with Jesus. If Jesus is treated as "the least of these," then whatever is done to the hungry and the oppressed is done to him. If Jesus rises up, the oppressed will rise up. If the established society oppresses, neglects, or crucifies the least of these, this society will be held accountable. So when we look at that empty cross, we should get a little nervous. It symbolizes that "the least" are alive and fermenting a resurrection among those who are dead in oppression, the ones who have had no say in their lives. And now the crucial question: *Why do the innocent suffer?* The answer is, for the same reason that Jesus suffered. Because *people,* not God, decided to make or let them suffer. That's bad news, on the one hand, especially for those with the power to prevent the slaughter of the innocent. But it's good news, on the other hand, because if people can decide to oppress others and to endure oppression, they can also decide to change it. *Fatalism is the only enemy.* If those who are lost in the despair of oppression are there because of the human greed of others, rather than the fatalism of a vengeful God, then they have hope in the resurrection.

The least will rise from the dead and take the power that is theirs. "Whenever man is being oppressed and destroyed, there God is being crucified and killed. But in the context of hope, suffering loses its power to draw man to despair, and becomes the fertilizing No from which the powers of bondage are destroyed for the sake of a new tomorrow liberation."†

Jesus' death and resurrection are both a private and a public matter. Good Friday and Easter are both rituals of personal faith and social hope. If the innocent dead have escaped their tomb, then God is able to upset any social oppression which tries to keep it closed.

---

*Rubem Alves, *A Theology of Human Hope* (Washington: Corpus Books, 1969), pp. 113–14.
†Ibid, p. 132.

Theological Term	Individual	Interpersonal	Intergroup
Crucifixion	His death for me	Death of the old self	Murder of the innocent
Resurrection	He overcomes death for me	The spirit rises in us	The least *up*rise

6. Sin as Dominance and Dependence

Of all the common theological terms, sin is the most privatized and the most trivialized. On the private level it is too often interpreted as naughtiness and the basically innocent pastime of impish, fun-loving people. It is seen as an irreverent disobedience of the boy/girl scout code of being honest, trustworthy, brave, clean, reverent, etc. Most reflective church people do go beyond this naive notion, however, into an understanding of the deeper forms of painful self-deception and subtle destructiveness into which people in their weak moments descend. Sins are often interpreted psychologically as any number of efforts to escape from reality, to hide and mask one's true self. The ancient seven deadly sins of gluttony, covetousness, envy, sloth, pride, anger, and lust have been diluted by modern psychology. So the anxiety and destructiveness of self-delusion and bad faith have become the central themes of existential psychoanalysis.

Emptiness, meaninglessness, and despair have become the modern "sins" of more sophisticated private religion. Existential anxiety has become a religious category for sin as we seek deeper and deeper into our psyches for a center of meaning, an inner peace away from a frantic, hassled daily life.

Many church people have found peace in small-group human growth activities. The anxiety is relieved by the sharing of one's private fears, pains, and joys with others who have similar experiences. The trusting and loving community becomes a warm family where one can grow and flourish.

Sin in this context tends to be seen less as personal anxiety and more as that which prevents one from trusting others. Sin is that which keeps us apart and builds suspicion. Sin is defensively holding back your true feelings and harboring hatreds and resentments. It is playing games and masking your private self. It is refusing to share who you are and judging and condemning others for sharing themselves. Sin is what prevents a loving community from developing this interpersonal perspective.

Sin takes on a much different meaning in a social large-group or intergroup context. Instead of the alienated self or the mistrusting small group, the *conditions* of a society become the focus of sin and evil. Individual people and interpersonal associations are not seen as the main source of sin. Rather, the evil social conditions make the private sin almost inevitable, or at least understandable. Social conditions of oppression, exploitation, and injustice turn individuals into dominating oppressors or dependent victims. The basic struggle between these two groups is over who will have the power to make the decisions and rules for the society.

The way this works out, of course, is very complex. As we noted earlier, the dominant and dependent groups need each other. Both are responsible for the social conditions, the dominant group for its sin of arrogance and pride (to use traditional theological language) and the dependent group for its sloth and aimlessness. Each group's sin exacerbates the other's. For example, growing up in the South one would hear, over and over, white people putting down Blacks for their presumed laziness. Since there was so little reward for them in work, it is amazing that Blacks worked as hard as they did. Nevertheless, it did not matter how little or how much work was actually done for the whites, it was never enough. The social structure was such that a white would often make the contradictory statements that "they are lazy" and that he or she (the white) had to work "like a nigger." The facts did not matter, because the whole social condition made this happen. Whites could order, intimidate, and exploit Blacks with impunity. But Blacks also could drive whites into a frenzy by refusing to cooperate, by playing irresponsible, by disappearing at a crucial time, by generally fouling up the work to be done, by saying yes and acting no. In a word, Blacks used what little power they had to sabotage the machinery of the social structure. If whites could intimidate Blacks physically, Blacks could undermine whites psychically. If whites could rant, rage, and rule, Blacks could act indecisive, aimless, disorganized, and incapable of taking anything and doing anything the way whites wanted it to be done.

This subtle use of the power of noncooperation is extensively analyzed by Gene Sharp,* who lists

*See *The Politics of Nonviolent Action* (Boston: Porter Sargent, 1973), pp. 285–347.

over one hundred types of political, economic, and social acts of noncooperation. He points out how Black slaves would flee, leaving the planter with his unpicked harvest, and then negotiate through other slaves for better working conditions as terms for his return.

Dependent behavior is exercised every day by children, who are forever calling a work slowdown or "playing dumb" to parents' orders. Women are trained so well in the high art of dependent behavior that sometimes a socially dependent woman can become personally dominant in a marriage relationship, even though a society still bars her from many positions of responsibility.

The role of the dominant group in any society is obvious. Rooted in the basic sin of pride (that is, like Adam and Eve, playing God), a dominant group simply assumes its superiority and teaches this assumption to its children and to the dependent group. A dominant group has overwhelming power to rule and to decide the fate of the dependent group. The latter can only undermine it, and then usually at great loss to itself.

The tragedy of this social sin is that since we are often blind to our social conditions ("Men wear blinders. They seldom see beyond their feed bags," said Buckminster Fuller), we actually believe the false consequences of these social sins. The powerful believe they are superior, and the powerless believe they are inferior. This dominant/dependent behavior thus constantly reinforces itself with the social-control mechanisms: That's Life, Blame the Victim, Follow the Leader, etc. These are social *sins* that play out the *sin* of dominance/dependence.

The tragic consequences of this belief are seen in the lives of whole tribes and cultures and in society's classes and economic groups. Without the opportunity to make their own decisions and order and rule their own lives according to their own cultural heritage, people are degraded to becoming the pathetic beggars and cowardly servants of a dominant culture. Travel to most of the southern hemisphere will reveal how colonial empires have ravaged not only the natural resources of Africa, Asia, and South America but also the psychic makeup of the people, whose heritage and culture have been stolen, degraded, or wiped out. The misery of the American Indian, for example, is beyond measure and beyond our ability to face or even begin to account for.

The ravaged consciousness that follows from such imperial conquests of cultures make of whole people "cultures of silence," as Paulo Freire calls them. They have been so exploited that they hardly have the will or the ability to act on their own even if they have the chance. They are easy prey to the cheap trinkets of a dominating imperial group. Being denied the right to set their own course in life and to decide for themselves, that ability almost atrophies out of nonuse. The overt violence that is inspired by oppressive conditions becomes covert violence in a dependent person. As Bernard LaFayette said once, "Apathy is internal violence."

In industrialized societies, people become dependent on a labor/money economy and lose the ability to produce their own food, shelter, and energy. But the most painful result of the sin of dominance/dependence is the loss of the ability to decide and rule oneself—the loss of freedom. The epitome of this loss is seen in the child of hunger who has a permanently damaged brain because of malnutrition, a lost soul for whom the sin of dominance must account.

The theological terms "pride" and "sloth" also apply on an individual, interpersonal *and* intergroup level. In the past, we have either quietly set these aside or perceived them only as private sins. But they apply in large groups also, and they can be illuminated by the intergroup relationship of dominance/dependence, dominance being the prideful attempt to play God by having too much power and dependence being the slothful attempt to deny power.

Theological Term	Individual	Interpersonal	Intergroup
Sin Pride	Disobey personal code Bad faith	Mistrust of others Condemning others	Conditions of oppression Dominance
Sloth	Irresponsibility	Defensiveness	Dependence
General secular barriers	Ego defense mechanisms	Games people play	Social control mechanisms

7. Repentance as Reparation and Courage

The Gospel of Mark begins with the preaching of John the Baptist and Jesus calling people to repent of their sins. There is a persistent call throughout the Bible to turn away from unrighteousness and toward a godly life. Repentance is a process of turning over values, life goals, and behavior. Repentance is the reversal of direction from sin to right living, according to traditional religious language.

Now the issue is, What does this mean to us in our daily life? How is it translated, if it is, to the common discourse we use with each other? Each level of private or group consciousness translates it differently or uses some parallel terminology, depending on its understanding of what it means to repent.

On the level of individual religion, sin is either seen trivially as breaking a moral code or more profoundly as existential bad faith. To repent of these is to face the facts, confess guilt, experience remorse, and resolve to keep the moral code or live in good faith, in authenticity.

On the level of the family or other small groups, repentance means to overcome estrangement from the group, to change one's mistrust and one's judging and defensive attitudes. To move from estrangement to belongingness is to repent of mistrust. It is to live openly and free of fear and the suspicion of others. When it comes to large groups, repentance is quite different because large groups don't have the same kind of conscious guilt and remorse that individuals do.* There are, however, types of mass group awareness. Carl Jung called this the "collective unconscious." We do know of whole societies, such as Nazi Germany, which get caught up in a mass hysteria. Indeed, any nation at war experiences collective hatreds, revenge, guilt, remorse, pity, and other emotions usually only attributed to individual persons.

Thus, repentance on a large-group level is possible. For example, postwar Germany has paid reparations to countries. Volunteers from Germany worked in Israeli kibbutzim as public forms of repentance. Equal employment legislation, affirmative action programs, and college admission and labor hiring on a compensatory quota system are all forms of social repentance or reparation for past injustices. The Thanksgiving basket, the old Christmas bonus, and all kinds of charities arise out of unfair social conditions about which the dominant group expresses personal concern or remorse. Indeed, many uses of charity which only

"Band Aid" the symptom of a social problem often help the remorseful dominant group repent even if the help for the dependent group is questionable. Charity can help continue the dependence. However, if it is seen as a group reparation rather than the personal generosity of the person in the dominant party, then the gift changes its meaning completely. It becomes an obligation due the dependent group rather than the largesse of the dominant one.

This idea of repentance as reparation applies, however, only to the arrogance and violence of a dominant group. How does a dependent group repent of sloth, aimlessness, indecisiveness, and cowardice? Obviously the way to turn around cowardice is to stand up, make decisions, and brave the consequences. To repent of sloth or dependence is to take hold of one's history, heritage, and culture and begin to celebrate, honor, and cherish one's group identity. It is to say, "My group (Black, female, youth, Asian, Red, Chicano, worker, farmer, New Yorker) is beautiful." To repent of aimlessness and indecision is to begin to aim and define the direction of a group's life. It is to take charge of who we are in an independent way. To repent of dependence is to make a declaration of independence from a group's colonial patron.

In Western societies we have focused more on the sin of *commission*—that is, aggression against others. Consequently, leaders have often stressed the need to repent of anger, ill feelings, and hostility. This is appropriate on a personal level for those who commit such sins. But it does not apply to dependent groups who avoid conflict, the sin of *omission*.

The Indian who has been taught to be ashamed of his or her culture does not need to repent of the sin of pride. Indeed, personal repentance complicates the issues of group sin. This person bears no guilt because ancestors were exploited. It is the group or tribe's duty to persist and maintain its proud identity and to seek to live by its own choices.

Jesus preached repentance to the scribes, Pharisees, and lawyers, the dominant groups in his society. But he also preached repentance to the woman caught in adultery (John 8:1-11) and the crippled man at the pool of Bethzatha (John 5). One was about to become the victim of a stoning, the other was bound to his stretcher and had given up hope of being healed. To both he said, "Sin no more." How could a cripple sin? Apparently his sin was that of giving up hope. It was not clear that he

---

*Paul Tillich says, "Social groups are power groups with no personal center as individuals have." (*Morality and Beyond* [New York: Harper & Row, 1963], p. 95.) Persons who lead and are members of groups keep changing. However, tradition and culture as well as the "collective unconscious" give groups a cohesive, if not personal, center.

even wanted to be healed. So Jesus asks him if he wants it. In response, the man tries to excuse himself (rather than saying, "Of course I do"). The sin of omission, of neglect, of sloth or dependence must be repented of, just as the sin of pride or dominance.

Group repentance does not require that all individuals put on sackcloth and ashes and go through periods of remorse. Rather, such repentance takes the form of reparation by the dominant group so that a social injustice is corrected. For the dependent group, it takes the form of courageous acts of independence. It means a redistributing of power, a sharing of it by the dominant group and an assuming of it by the dependent group.

Theological Term	Individual	Interpersonal	Intergroup
Repentance	Remorse	Becoming open	Reparation and courage

8. Salvation as Liberation

Salvation is a rescue operation by which one is delivered from some form of bondage. It is an act of God's grace, which we cannot control but one in which we must cooperate. The motto of the Protestant Reformation was, "We are saved by grace through faith." Thus, rescue is deeply personal, as it was for Martin Luther, who went through years of personal anxiety over the question of how he could be saved by works of religious practice. Luther concluded that salvation cannot be earned but must be received by faith. This thought started the Reformation.

Along with many other forces, this thought also encouraged a very private view of salvation. When Protestantism proclaimed the right of the individual conscience to stand before God, it not only shook the foundations of the church, it also made salvation a private matter between one human conscience and God rather than a community affair of the church. This had to be done, and we are the beneficiaries of this four-hundred-year-old event. However, the private rescue of one soul by God is not the total picture of salvation.

Salvation cannot be divorced from one's community or one's social predicament. A friend drove into Boston one night, parked his car on the street, and went for dinner and a movie, unaware that a snowstorm was on the way. When he came out, he found his car almost buried in a snowbank. He had

no shovel, so he started digging out with his hands. After a while he felt someone was watching him. When he looked up, he saw a man holding some papers. The man then handed him one of the papers. It was a religious tract. The man said nothing, but the tract asked my snowbound friend, "Are you saved?"

Obviously, the bondage of my friend had more to do with snow than with the personal sin from which the stranger sought to dislodge him. But private religion sometimes misses such an obvious point. Salvation is a community as well as a personal affair.

Even if the church had lapsed into selling indulgences as a work of salvation and had corrupted much of the notion of salvation by grace, it was still the church community, a group of people, that gave Luther and gives us these words of grace and salvation. We experience the support of our friends in grief and sickness and throughout the crises of our lives. And it does not take away from the saving grace of God to say that such community support "saved" us or helped save us from some forms of hell. What it does is strengthen the forms of community.

The interpersonal church-family support is a constant help in the process of our salvation. God uses each of us to help one another, and in the process the group itself is filled with spirit and saved from itself and other alien forces.

Again the question is, How can a large group be saved? This is an unusual concept for us to deal with. There is no doubt about personal salvation. The freeing of a family from alcoholism or divorce is clear enough and obviously an act of God's saving grace. But how does God rescue a whole people from bondage? Is this part of the Christian catechism?

We have a hard time perceiving the salvation of a whole culture or society, because we think of salvation in private terms. Also, we assume that bondage, barriers, or sin are only personal vices. But the bondage or sin of a large group is, as we have seen, a social condition in which a dominant group controls another and the dependent group submits. To save such a society is to let loose forces by which this structure is turned around. Ideally, the salvation of a society is one in which the dependent group declares its independence and the dominant group relinquishes its power so that all people move toward an interdependent society of equals.

But this is only the ideal process. In history, dominant groups rarely ever let go of power. It must be taken. Pharaoh would not release the children of Israel, but God saved them anyway. This does not necessarily mean that violent revolution is inevitable either. In this case, the Hebrew people did not take up arms in battle, they ran.

A whole nation of people were saved from the bondage of slavery, and no mention is made in Exodus of private conscience, faith, or personal salvation except for that of Moses. God rescued an entire people, and God can do the same again. Indeed, whenever a dependent group is liberated from domination and dependence, it is not bad theology to detect God actively at work. Certainly, the Bible is full of God's liberating of whole groups of people. God not only saved a city like Nineveh when it repented of its sin, God also delivered Israel over to the hand of her enemies when no righteousness could be found. In either case a whole nation was saved or condemned.

Liberation theology is all about the process of rescuing Third World people out of colonialism and economic bondage. The process is a process of liberation or the rescuing of a large group of people. That process is also the burden of this book. As we move from consciousness of social conditions to visioning alternatives to exercising power to change, we are trying to understand the relationship of dominant and dependent groups and how to move that relationship to one of interdependence. In a word, we are seeking social salvation, currently known as liberation.

Theological Term	Individual	Interpersonal	Intergroup
Salvation	Soul rescuing	Individuals restored to the group	Liberation of a people

9. Morality as Standards for Using Power Without Corruption

What is immoral for you? What is it that you would never do? Where would you draw the line on your "ethics?"* Where would you draw it for others?

*We will use the word morality to mean the standards of behavior called for within a certain culture or tradition. For purposes of this book, that tradition is the Western Christian tradition. "Moral" is an adjective which describes acts performed according to, or in violation of, these standards. Ethics is the study or science of morality although in popular use, which we quote here, ethics is used interchangeably with morality.

An example of some moral wisdom that applies generally is found in the questions we can ask about a particular moral decision: (1) What are the basic values I am serving and seeking? That is, what are my religious commitments? What gods or God will this choice honor? (2) What wisdom from the past bears on this choice, such as moral codes, customs, and, most of all, biblical principles? (3) What are all the facts and peculiarities of the present choice that have a bearing now? (4) What future consequences are likely to result from the choice? (5) How urgent is the choice at this time? (6) What priority does this choice have for me relative to other choices?

Another important distinction is between individual, interpersonal, and intergroup morality. Like our other theological terms, the focus is different simply because the crowds are bigger.

First, personal morality relates to my basic values, my gods, or God. Every choice I make serves these values one way or another. So morality (the standards for acting out one's values) is vitally connected to religion (the values as such). Personal moral choices have to do with the effects these choices will have on *me.* If I tell a lie, will the consequences be worse for me or better? If I overindulge in food or drink (gluttony), will I have to pay for it and how much? What will varying forms of sexual activity do to me? Will they corrupt me in some way? Which will, which won't, and which might? Every profession has some code of "ethics" that involves many personal aspects. The scholar must be accurate, the teacher prepared for class, the athlete in good physical condition, the doctor up to date on treatments. This personal morality does have effects on others, but the prime results of obedience or disobedience are personal. If I drink too much, I will suffer more than anyone else. So we have moral codes, especially for the young, to help them learn to care for themselves.

Second, interpersonal morality is closely connected to personal morality. My smoking results in worse health for me, but it is also bad for those around me who have to breathe it. Morality on this level is easily confused with etiquette and manners (aesthetics), on the one hand, and law on the other. However, morality is the basic standard for how all people are treated. It is the condition and criterion for all behavior. From morality, then, we develop the helpful rules to protect ourselves and to respect and affirm other people, called manners. In addition, laws are written to codify certain moral standards by which lawmakers seek to order society.

Interpersonal morality deals with our basic behavior toward other people. The *law* punishes us if we attack another person and are found guilty, but *morality* is preventive. It restrains us because of our prior standard of behavior, irrespective of the law. Professional "ethics" are rarely codified by social laws, but they are standards that professionals and guilds use to keep their members in line. Business "ethics" are meant to keep unsavory practices from getting out of hand and causing the whole profession to suffer. However, professional and business "ethics" rarely deal with broad issues of social morality. Interpersonal morality is a help *within* a group. It does not apply outside or between groups. This is our third point.

This is where intergroup or social ethics comes in. To begin with an example, let's say that the only doctor in a small remote town is personally upright and responsible, is up to date in his practice, is objective and friendly toward patients. But what if that doctor, in collaboration with other doctors and with the consent of the American Medical Association, decides to charge $75 for a five-minute office visit, $800 for a physical exam, $2,000 for an appendectomy, and $10,000 for child delivery?

Where does the accountability rest? It is probably not illegal. The doctor is certainly personally moral and even genuinely affectionate toward his patients. He is taking all that money in a legally approved way. But is it moral? Since patients have no choice but to pay or suffer, they go to the bank and borrow money at high interest rates to pay medical bills. Where does morality come in here? This aspect of morality is often ignored. Cases of mercy killing, as another example, are usually debated on personal and legal grounds. To ask about the *cost* of prolonged treatment (which can come to millions of dollars for a family, whether it is rich or poor) is considered irrelevant. But it is one important factor of social morality.

The point is that neither personal nor interpersonal morality, neither manners, etiquette, nor law, covers all aspects of a moral issue. That's why we must have criteria, standards, moral guidelines for relations between *groups* of people—in this case doctors and patients but also in virtually every area of life. There are no laws governing many aspects of international relations or foreign trade. Laws that are meant to protect minorities and the poor are often ignored. Equal treatment is guaranteed under the law, but money can buy easier sentences for rich people. Out-of-court settlement and plea bargaining are common practice. It's legal, but is it moral?

What is to prevent the rule of might makes right in large social groups? What will restrain the rich from exploiting the poor? What are sensible criteria for corporate accountability? Who enforces the international laws of war? At present, these international laws amount to "victor's ethics," in which the conqueror condemns the conquered (as in Nuremberg, Germany) but ignores the same principles in Vietnam.

Social morality tries to set standards for behavior in this large-group realm whereby the negative consequences are reduced for *all* people. It tries to restrain the code of might makes right and enforce a right-makes-right principle.

Something tells us that all children should have enough to eat whoever they are. Social morality speaks to this.

Something tells us it is not right for the United States to give food for peace to well-off political allies and to ignore starving nations who would not politically benefit us. Social morality speaks to this.

Something tells us that it is not right to sell or give away military weapons to every possible country. Social morality speaks to this.

All these kinds of issues fall between the cracks of laws and conventional, personal morality. But more people are hurt and killed because moral restraint does not protect them enough in this large-group dimension.

Intergroup morality seeks to overcome the dominant/dependent relationship, to promote just and peaceful social conditions, and to reduce the harm done by the social sins that powerlessness and the concentration of power result in. Social morality seeks to counter the games pharaohs play and help the powerless become conscious of their conditions, envision alternatives, and use power to defend themselves and to obtain their rights and equality.

Social morality sets standards by which power can be redistributed. It seeks to prevent corruption, not because corruption is a personal moral issue but because corruption makes people powerless. In this intergroup view, moral purity takes on a whole new meaning. One avoids gluttony, drunkenness, drugs, and promiscuity because this is good personal morality; one also avoids them because these things make people dependent, powerless, disorganized, indecisive, and corrupt. If power corrupts, so does powerlessness.

Social morality, unlike personal morality, sees how colonial empires enforce decadence on their colonies by pushing drugs (opium) in China, alcohol in Indochina, and weapons throughout the world. It sees how dominant groups actually benefit from the dependency that bad health practices and mind-changing drugs and food cause. Colonial systems function on the ability of the imperialist to keep the colonists diverted from their misery. The French did this in their colonies and made money on alcohol at the same time. Drunken Indians don't go on warpaths. Roman soldiers, given bread and circuses, don't mutiny. Consumers, lost in shopping centers, don't organize against inflation.

In short, from this perspective moral purity is important *not* because of abstract laws or heavenly record keeping but because corruption makes people vulnerable to exploitation. Bad health and mental dullness render people powerless. The liberation of oppressed, dependent people requires clear minds, hard work, and disentangled lives. Persons corrupted by materialism of any kind are trapped in the fleshpots of Egypt. The ten commandments given on Mount Sinai were not given only to help individuals or simply to encourage persons to cooperate with each other. Help and cooperation are good and necessary. But the ten commandments had to be observed to rid God's chosen people from the enslaved minds and spirits of the brickyards of slavery. These are socially significant, moral rules, because they were necessary for the people if they ever hoped to get out of the desert into the land of milk and honey.

Theological Term	Individual	Interpersonal	Intergroup
Morality and Ethics	Standards for self-morality	Standards for ethical interpersonal behavior	Social ethics— Standards for the use of power without corruption

Now we will put this theological survival kit together into one package:

Theological Term	Individual	Interpersonal	Intergroup
God	Father	Love	Power
Jesus	My savior who loves me	Our savior in our midst	The least of these

Holy Spirit	Mystery within	Internal group spirit	Empowering spirit
Crucifixion	His death for me	Death of the old self	Murder of the innocent
Resurrection	He overcomes death for me	The spirit rises in us	Uprise of the least
Sin	Disobey personal code	Mistrust of others	Conditions of oppression
Pride	Arrogance	Condemning others	Dominance
Sloth	Irresponsibility	Defensiveness	Dependence
General secular barriers	Ego defense mechanisms	Games people play	Social control mechanisms
Repentance	Remorse	Becoming open	Reparation and courage
Salvation	Soul rescuing	Individuals restored to the group	Liberation of a people
Morality	Standards for self	Standards for interpersonal behavior	Standards for the use of power without corruption

3. SOCIAL VISION

These nine theological terms are the criteria to be used to distinguish a vision from a nightmare. These theological terms have direct bearing upon one's social vision, and one's vision directly applies to one's daily choices and life's work. Here are a few of the more obvious implications for this theological understanding for a Christian vision that encompasses intergroup concerns.

1. If God is the power of mystery in all life, then all our visions are tentative; all things have uncertainty, mystery, about them. This leaves no room for absolutes, for fanatical, self-righteous movements.

2. If God is the power of mystery in all life, then we have cause for great hope. This leaves room for miracles, for sudden collapses of oppressive regimes, and for new courage to act.

3. If Jesus is the Christ, the "least," then the downtrodden are God's chosen. This means we should have a healthy (but unromantic) bias toward the oppressed.

4. If the Holy Spirit is working from within us, lifting up the poor in spirit, then we should expect the

unexpected. This mystical reality in all persons demands that all persons be honored and treated as ends, never as means.

5. If the crucifixion is the result of human decision, then people are accountable for all such deaths and the slaughter of the innocents can be stopped. This means our vision should include the care of the weak and innocent.

6. If the resurrection means the uprising of the least, then our vision should rise to the occasion.

7. If sin is a social condition of dominance and dependence, then our vision includes the interdependence of all peoples.

8. If repentance is reparation from the dominant groups and courage by the dependent groups, then our vision should include a redistribution and equalization of wealth and power.

9. If salvation is the process of liberation, then our vision should include the opportunity of all people to meet their basic physical and spiritual needs.

10. If morality means the standards for the use of power to obtain liberation without corruption, then our vision should include the means for resisting corruption.

These are only a few implications of how a clear theological understanding can inform our vision and help us distinguish it from nightmares and fanatical schemes. These only refer to the intergroup social vision. A more inclusive vision will allow for more needs of individuals and account for the benefits of the small group.

The *social* vision focuses more on the future, however. Hope is its central religious attitude. Small groups are drawn together by love, and the individual lives in faith. If individual religion seeks right belief (orthodoxy) and small-group religion seeks right feeling, the large-group religion seeks right action (orthopraxis). All three are vital: faith, hope, and love; belief, feeling, and action. But we will never begin to move toward a social vision relying only on the benefits of private religion. This has been our main source of despair in the past. There is no need to wait until everyone loves one another and has personal faith in our God before we begin to seek justice and a vision of shalom. This personal righteousness will probably never happen because of personal sin. If hatred, anger, distrust, and all personal sin were abolished, we most likely would still have social sin running rampant. But social sin can be controlled. Dominance and dependence, war, poverty, and oppression

are not inevitable. They can be changed. Therefore, hope guides our vision.

Finally, we all must have our say in what a vision contains, because if someone is left out of the decision-making and the rule-making, then the basic respect for persons implied in Christianity is lost from the beginning. However, we can share our visions with each other and constantly improve them. Here is one vision that a group of us put together at a conference. It is only a brief sample to encourage others to do their own visioning.

A Vision

We envision a time of shalom when persons and nature live in harmony, infused with the spirit of their Creator. In that vision we see:

an "abundant life" for all, in which we consume less and enjoy it more because the basic needs of all persons are met;

the "dividing wall of hostility" broken down between persons and nature, rich and poor, male and female, nations, races, and cultures— a time when each is honored for its own uniqueness, and all are enabled to contribute their special gifts;

a time when people will have both political and economic rights to life, liberty, and self-reliance;

a time when persons will have the minimum goods and knowledge and health to care for their own basic needs;

a world in which each person will have a voice in the decisions that affect her or him and in which all persons, institutions, and corporate bodies are accountable for their actions;

a time when energy resources and their production, distribution, and use will be completely safe, nonpolluting, renewable, and widely distributed throughout the world;

a time when the ecosystem will be again in balance and waste will not exist as all products are used and recycled;

a time when all the creativity of humanity will be tapped and valued in its expression—in work, art, and recreation that serve the common good;

a time in which all human decisions and relationships will be freely made and sustained in social and personal covenants of health and wholeness.

III. USING POWER

OVERVIEW

The following exercises are intended to mobilize people and to make them aware of the hard disciplines of action. The abilities to act deliberately and to enjoy small victories are requirements for making a difference.

Winners and Losers intends to help people locate themselves in a social world and to locate victims of injustice. Most important is the need to stop playing a winner/helper role and begin to define one's social role as ally in coalition with the victims. This moves acts of helping out of the realm of charity and dependence to acts of justice and interdependence.

Planning for Hope helps people get themselves together to act on a problem. The exercises on Beautania intend to give people experience in the use of power in an exaggerated and rigid social structure. The ability to name the tactics of power politics helps people to avoid being deceived by them. The welfare exercises enable people to experience a new look at taxes and welfare and to plan a congressional visit.

What's to Be Done? intends to encourage people to action by selecting from and experiencing the enormous number of possible nonviolent tactics available to them. The last exercise, Doing It, encourages people to organize, confront a landlord, and win a rent action. Thereby a group can learn to exercise its rights and work together toward justice and toward shalom in its community and the world beyond it.

The background readings in this section bring us face to face with some hard realities. If, in fact, we are about the task of social change toward a more peaceful, equitable and just society, then we must take into account the traps and pitfalls along the way. Social-Control Mechanisms unearth many of those stumbling blocks. We must also be alerted to most judicious use of our own individual and corporate power. The Church and the Use of Power delineate those possibilities. Questions of Power gives us a tool to use as we both plan and act for justice and peace.

EXERCISES IN USING POWER

WINNERS AND LOSERS   **PART 1 AWARENESS/ANALYSIS**

PURPOSE:
To help people define themselves in society and to encourage a cooperative approach to assisting others, whereby equals assist equals in a common need.

ASSUMPTIONS:
People rarely perceive themselves in their social roles. They also have different social roles in different circumstances.
Role definition helps people understand, perceive options, and begin to change their social conditions.

PREPARATION:
Some people will be in more than one role. Be prepared to have them define which roles seem to dominate. Read Background Readings, on Using Power. Note coalition principle.

TIME:
45 minutes

MATERIALS:
Newsprint
Pencils

PROCEDURE:
1. Draw two parallel vertical lines on four sheets of newsprint. Write "Winner" at the top of one line and "Helper" at the top of the other; write "Loser" and "Ally" at the bottom of those lines; e.g.,

2. Write one of the following roles on each one of the four sheets.
   Global Citizen
   U.S. Citizen
   Consumer
   Employee (or other occupation, including student)
3. Have participants sign their initials at points along each line where they would place themselves, one sheet at a time. For example, have each person initial where they feel they are as a Global Citizen on the winner-loser scale, and then on the helper-ally scale.
4. After all have initialed their place on each line on the first sheet, ask them to explain why. Then repeat the initialing on the next sheet as U.S. Citizen, etc. Repeat discussion each time. Take about 10 minutes on each sheet.
5. Conclude with a discussion of which role is more useful, helper or ally. Where possible, relate the discussion to the reading.

SUPPORTIVE RESOURCES:
Background Readings on Using Power (pages 96–109)

PLANNING FOR HOPE

PURPOSE:
To help people think, organize, and act according to a common plan.

ASSUMPTIONS:
Social change requires considerable planning and deliberate follow-through and evaluation.
The better defined the plans are, the more cohesion there is in a group; and the more cohesion, the more easily one's goals are obtained.

PREPARATION:
Read Questions of Power: A Checklist, in Background Readings. You might consider rewriting "The Committee Met" to represent a problem or issue closer to the participants' experience. The important point of the story is the style and movement (or lack of movement!).

TIME:
1 hour

MATERIALS:
The Committee Met, a short story
Copies of A Simple Planning Tool

PROCEDURE:

A. Beginning: *(15 minutes)*
1. Ask people to listen or look for the flaws in this story, read "The Committee Met" aloud or have a group role-play it or duplicate it for individual responses.
2. Discuss what's wrong in the story. Have everyone participate. Ask if they have ever served on such a committee.

B. Practice Planning: *(25 minutes)*
1. Have participants gather in pairs. Pass out planning questionnaire, A Simple Planning Tool.
2. Work through questionnaire in pairs. Fill it out. Try to isolate an issue small enough to be able to work on.

C. Report Back: *(20 minutes)*
1. Have three or four read their plans. Provide enough time for the groups to question and respond.
2. Conclude with a reading of Matthew 25:1-13, the foolish maidens.

SUPPORTIVE RESOURCES:
Questions of Power: A Checklist (pages 106–09)
A Simple Planning Tool (pages 129–30)

The Committee Met

WHAT'S WRONG WITH THIS SCENE?

The committee met and concluded that something had to be done about bribery, fraud, kickbacks, and general corruption in the mayor's office. When his horse won the lottery for the sixth straight time, it looked suspicious. When the party put the horse on the ballot, people got incensed. When it won a council seat, they called a meeting.

The good government committee met for three hours in the library basement. Everybody was furious and agreed that corruption had to be rooted out of the administration.

The press picked up the cries of anguish. The indignant citizens witnessed to one abuse after another. "Throw the bum out" rang out from the card catalogue area. Babies cried and dogs barked most of the night. Something should be done. It was unanimous; the motion carried. The gavel fell and the "Star-Spangled Banner" was sung. Surely a clean sweep was in store for the gang at city hall.

Write your answer below to what is wrong with this scene:

The answer is below (don't peek!).

This scene has everybody aroused but nothing but nothing was decided, nothing was planned, and nothing will get done.

82

BEAUTIES, MIDDIES, AND YUCKIES   PART 1 AWARENESS/ANALYSIS

PURPOSE:
To experience, detect, and analyze some of the methods or tools of power used between oppressors and the oppressed.

ASSUMPTIONS:
There are certain identifiable methods that are used in societies in order to maintain an oppressive structure. Educators for social change need the ability to see, understand, and deal with these methods.

PREPARATION:
Prepare to help people to play out their roles.
Prepare people to take some abuse in a role play.
Read Background Readings on Using Power.
Be sure to have all the paper cleaning towels under game leader's control.

TIME:
1½ hours

MATERIALS:
Name tags and pins
Instructions for Beauties, Middies, and Yuckies

Paper cleaning towels, 56 of them
Copies of Spotting Power Politics for each participant

PROCEDURE:

A. Beginning: *(15 minutes)*
1. People count off in threes as Beauties, Middies, and the Yuckies. All make group name tags and pin them on. "Hello! I'm a _____."
2. Have two "neutral" volunteer observers to help monitor the project.
3. The project is to beautify the palace in Beautania where the Beauties live. This project is announced. The palace can be made beautiful (cleaned, decorated, and straightened) only by the use of the cleaning towels.
4. Ask each group (Beauties, Middies, and Yuckies) to gather in separate rooms and await instructions.
5. Instructions are given to each group—Beauties first, Middies second, and Yuckies last, after a 5-minute delay and appropriate insults. Beauties get 50 cleaning towels, Middies 5, Yuckies 1.
6. Each group gets into roles and plots their strategies. [Beauties plan to use their power, i.e., their monopoly of the towels, to get Middies to control the Yuckies' work.]

B. Playing the Simulation: *(45 minutes)*
These are the rules:
1. Beauty towels are all at once the medium of exchange, the tools for cleaning, and material for beautiful clothes and decorations.
2. Beauty towels can be earned in exchange for beautification work. They can also be rented for work to be done.
3. One beauty towel can be earned by saying "You are beautiful" ten times to the towel owner. If the owner likes your way of saying it, he or she can give it. It's not mandatory to give the towels.
4. Whoever has the most beauty towels at the end rules the palace, makes the decisions, and becomes beautiful.

C. Summary Discussion and Reflection: *(20 minutes)*
Immediately following the simulation it is important to spend time sharing feelings and insights related to the experience.
1. In plenary session the enabler, or simulation director, should lead the group in responding to the following questions:

What is it like to be a Beauty? a Middy? a Yucky?

What role did Middies have? Yuckies? Beauties?

Did you feel yucky and/or beautiful?

What does this experience say to you about roles in society?

Name some social values in our society that work like beauty towels.

How are society's values controlled?

2. Distribute copies of Spotting Power Politics. The instructions are included. *(5–10 minutes)* The point is to stimulate people's thinking and widen their perception. In plenary session discuss:

Are the social-control mechanisms accurate?

Have you experienced any of them?

Do you use any?

Can we live with these mechanisms? How?

Can we live without these mechanisms? How?

3. Have a Yucky read aloud Matthew 19:23-30.

SUPPORTIVE RESOURCES:
Spotting Power Politics (page 131)

Instructions for Beauties, Middies, and Yuckies

THE CASTE SYSTEM IN BEAUTANIA:

To Beauties
1. You are a proud group. Because of your beauty and noble blood, you believe you were born to rule and decide in Beautania. Naturally, things work well for you because you make the decisions according to your desires.

2. Your only burden is that lesser people have to be dealt with. The Middies usually do your bidding because they want to become beautiful. They control the Yuckies, who you believe were born to do manual labor.

3. You have control of the room to be cleaned and arranged and most of the beauty towels.

4. You must see that the room is beautified, although you cannot do it yourself; nor can you permit the Middies, much less the Yuckies, to make any decisions about how it is beautified.

5. You not only own most of the other beautifying equipment, but, because of your beauty, you use all the tools of power politics. They have practical use in helping you stay beautiful and in charge of the Middies and Yuckies.

6. You want the palace beautified, but you must be very, very careful who you let do it, and how many. The workers must be regulated, identified, instructed, and taxed. You own most of the beauty towels, so it is your right to rent them out for purposes of cleaning.

To Middies
1. You are the middle people in Beautania. You envy and respect the Beauties because, of course, they are beautiful. You are not (yet) beautiful but you aren't (praise beauty) yucky either.

2. You like the Beauties too (sometimes) because they let you into some of their life. You get to guard the doors and see that the Yuckies don't contaminate the Beauties' palace. You help them do manual labor and sometimes try to help them in your moments of compassion.

3. You could become a Beauty if you knew the secrets of power politics. Once in a while you get a glimpse of it, and you hope to piece it all together one day, if not for yourself, at least "for the kids."

To Yuckies
1. You, frankly, aren't much. But you do what you can or what you are told. You endure because there isn't much else and because one day you may become a Middy. Some Yuckies have made it.

2. You don't like being so yucky but there are compensations. You don't have to decide anything. Decisions are painful. You just do what you are told, i.e., manual labor. You are grateful sometimes for this but it's a bit insulting.

3. It's a great honor to enter the palace and, if chosen, you are flattered to be able to enter.

PURPOSE:
To experience, in microcosm, social stratification and the flow of power between the varying levels.

ASSUMPTIONS:
Social change happens in an interplay of power forces.
Oppressed people have power for this interplay if they unite.

PREPARATION:
Prepare 4 rooms.
Duplicate attachments.
Coach monitors on rules.
Request people to stick to the rules of the simulation or take the position of a silent observer.

TIME:
1¼ hours

MATERIALS:
Liberator's Tool Kit
Action Questionnaire
The Change Chart
4 rooms or 4 separate areas, one for each group and a "jail"

PROCEDURE:

A. Beginning: *(15 minutes)*
1. Explain the situation: as in "Beauties, Middies, and Yuckies," the social structure in Beautania is tight. All have their place, and that place is set by the rules and decisions of the Beauties. Now a particular problem has arisen to cause strife in Beautania, and the Beauties, of course, define all strife as bad and blame the Yuckies. The Middies usually do, too, but this is an exception. This strife is between Yuckies and Beauties, which is unheard of because usually only the Yuckies and Middies fight and the law only permits Yuckies to fight each other.

Now it seems that after some young Beauty boys chased down some young Middy girls, they also beat up some elderly Yucky men, just out of meanness. However, the situation now is that one Middy girl and one Yucky elder are in "protective custody."

The law says the attacker, not the victims, should be held responsible. All is very tense in Beautania. No one knows when they will be released. No one has seen them, and it is rumored that some are hurt and without medical attention, which Beauty jails never give (that's up to relatives). Bond is set for 10 beauty towels each.
2. Explain the rules:
Don't go outside the boundaries of the situation.
Write down and pass your moves to the monitors.
If a meeting is desired, tell monitor, who will negotiate it and then role play it.
Wait for written responses to your moves.
Celebrate small victories.

B. Simulation: *(45 minutes)*
1. Count off into three groups: Yuckies, Middies, and Beauties. Go to separate rooms to wait for instructions.
2. Ask for 3 observers to monitor each group.
3. Deliver instructions and beauty towels to each. Beauties get 50, Middies 10, Yuckies 1.

4. Monitors facilitate and arrange meetings and communiqués.

5. Volunteer one Middy "girl" and one Yucky "elder" (can be any age or sex) to go to jail. Guard is a Middy.

6. Groups write out moves to support their interests.

C. Discussion: *(15 minutes)*

1. Possible discussion questions:

What was it like to be a Yucky? Middy? Beauty?

Did Yuckies feel any power?

Did a coalition develop between Yuckies and Middies? If so, did it work? If not, why not?

Post the Change Chart. Can any of the actions taken be charted here? Is it helpful to see action in these categories? Reflect on how the power flowed. Did Yuckies gain any power? How would you apply the social strata of Beautania to your own?

How does a social structure affect cultural identity? pride?

How does change affect cultural unity?

2. Read Acts 16:16-39, Paul and Silas in prison.

Instructions for Yuckies Unite

TO YUCKIES

1. You are fed up. This may be the chance for change.
2. Note the options you have.
   a. Middy girls were attacked.
   b. Beauties broke their own law.
   c. Prison reform is ripe.
   d. Medical attention provides entrance into jail.
3. Read over Liberator's Tool Kit, The Change Chart, and A Simple Planning Tool. Get organized and act.
4. "Yuck is beautiful."
5. List demands.

TO MIDDIES

1. You are angry at the attack on Middy girls.
2. You believe it's unfair to jail the victims.
3. You are ready to join forces and act.
4. Read The Change Chart, Liberator's Tool Kit, and A Simple Planning Tool.
5. Make action plan.

TO BEAUTIES

1. Well, you are in a beautiful mess. You've got Yuckies and Middies with a common cause.
2. You know this, so you are ready to compromise on jail conditions and bond.
3. You will give in on almost anything except your basic control of the rules and decision-making and the balance of power you have kept between Yuckies and Middies.

SUPPORTIVE RESOURCES:

The Change Chart (page 132)
Liberator's Tool Kit (page 133)
A Simple Planning Tool (pages 129–30)
Spotting Power Politics (page 131)

PURPOSE:
To begin to look at welfare, tax incentives, loopholes, and benefits in a new way.
To help people discover where they benefit or lose from the tax rules.

ASSUMPTIONS:
To change society one must understand power.
To understand power one must understand who makes the rules and who makes the decisions.
To understand these rules and decisions one needs to know who directs the flow of money.

PREPARATION:
Read Philip Stern's article carefully before the session.
Have enough copies for only half the group.
Recognize that this is only the surface of a very large and complex problem. Fold copies of questionnaire on dotted line.
NOTE: Figures may vary slightly from these [1971] figures.

TIME:
1 hour

MATERIALS:
Copies of Tax Welfare Questionnaire
Copies of article by Philip M. Stern, "Uncle Sam's Welfare Program for the Rich"

PROCEDURE:

A. Beginning: *(25 minutes)*
 1. Have people fill in questionnaires individually and keep them folded until you signal that everyone is finished.
 2. Have people unfold questionnaires so they can discover their tax welfare.
 3. Permit free discussion about the meaning of tax welfare. Ask: How many guessed accurately? How far off? Distinguish "tax welfare" from welfare.

B. Test in Groups: *(15 minutes)*
 1. Have people count off in threes like this: "rich," "poor," "middle." The "rich," "poor," and "middle" gather in separate groups.
 2. Explain that there will be a simple test on the Stern article. Pass out copies of the Stern article to the rich first, one each, and tell them to begin reading. Slowly give the middle people one article for every two people. Let them start reading. When you run out of articles before you get to the poor, of course, you apologize for the oversight.
 3. Test question: Ask what Senator Russell Long says about welfare loafers, the answer should be given sternly and in the direction of the "poor." The completed questionnaire can be dropped or thrown on the floor in the "poor section."

C. Conclusion: *(5 minutes)*
 1. A concluding assembly of the whole group can begin as soon as each group cleans up its area.
 2. A final open discussion should reflect on this experience and share insights.

Tax Welfare Questionnaire

Instructions: 1. Keep page folded
2. Circle your income
3. Guess at your "tax welfare"

If your yearly family income is:	Your "tax welfare" is (guestimate)		Your "tax welfare" is
Over $1,000,000	_____	Fold	$720,000
$500–1,000,000	_____	back	$202,000
$100–500,000	_____	before	$ 41,000
$50–100,000	_____	answering	$ 12,000
$25–50,000	_____		$ 4,000
$15–25,000	_____		$ 1,200
$10–15,000	_____		$ 650
$5–10,000	_____		$ 340
$3–5,000	_____		$ 48
Under $3,000	_____		$ 16

If your yearly income is:	Your "tax welfare" from capital gains is (guestimate)	Your "tax welfare" from capital gains is
Over $1,000,000	_____	$641,000
$500–1,000,000	_____	$165,000
$100–500,000	_____	$ 23,000
$20–25,000	_____	$ 120
$5–10,000	_____	$ 8
$3–5,000	_____	$ 1

If your yearly income is	Your "tax welfare" if married is (guestimate)	Your "tax welfare" if married is
Under $3,000	_____	$ 0.00
$3–5,000	_____	$ 0.72
$5–10,000	_____	$ 24.00
$25–50,000	_____	$ 1,479.00
$100–500,000	_____	$ 8,212.00
Over $1,000,000	_____	$11,062.00

UNCLE SAM'S WELFARE PROGRAM FOR THE RICH*

Most Americans would probably be intensely surprised to find, in their morning newspaper, headlines such as this one: Congress Sets $16-Per-Year Welfare Rate for Poor Families, $720,000 for Multimillionaires. Or this one: Nixon Asks $103 Billion Budget Deficit, Doubling Previous Red-Ink Record.

The story behind the first of these headlines might read this way:

Washington, April 16—Congress completed action today on a revolutionary welfare program that, reversing traditional payment policies, awards huge welfare payments to the super-rich but grants only pennies per week to the very poor.

Under the program, welfare payments averaging some $720,000 a year will go to the nation's wealthiest families, those with annual incomes of over a million dollars.

For the poorest families, those earning $3,000 a year or less, the welfare allowance will average $16 a year, or roughly 30 cents a week.

The program, enacted by Congress in a series of laws over a period of years, has come to be called the Rich Welfare Program, after its principal sponsor, Senator Homer A. Rich. In a triumphant news conference, Senator Rich told newsmen that the $720,000 annual welfare allowance would give America's most affluent families an added weekly take home pay of about $14,000. "Or, to put it another way," the Senator said, "it will provide these families with about $2,000 more spending money every day."

The total cost of the welfare program, the most expensive in the nation's history, amounts to $77.3 billion a year.

Political analysts foresee acute discontent not only among the poor, but also among middle-income families making $10,000 to $15,000 a year. For them, welfare payments under the Rich plan will amount to just $12.50 a week, markedly less than the weekly $14,000 paid to the very rich.

Reporters asked Senator Rich whether wealthy families would be required to work in order to receive their welfare payments, a common eligibility requirement with many welfare programs. Senator Rich seemed puzzled by the question.

"The rich? Work?" he asked. "Why, it hadn't occurred to me." Congressional experts advised newsmen that the program contains no work requirement.*

Who gets how much of the "tax welfare" payments from the major "tax preferences"—the loopholes? Until recently, one could only make, at best, an educated guess. But in January, two tax experts at the Brookings Institution in Washington, D.C., Joseph A. Perchman and Benjamin Okner, made a computer analysis of information from actual tax returns (furnished on computer tape, without taxpayer names, by the IRS). Using this data, plus other information from economic surveys, they came up with answers that might astound or even anger, put-upon taxpayers.

On a per-family basis, a breakdown of the average tax savings of Americans—our "tax welfare" program—looks like this:

Yearly Income	Yearly "Tax Welfare"
Over $1,000,000	$720,000
$500–1,000,000	$202,000
$100–500,000	$ 41,000
$50–100,000	$ 12,000
$25–50,000	$ 4,000
$15–25,000	$ 1,200
$10–15,000	$ 650
$5–10,000	$ 340
$3–5,000	$ 48
Under $3,000	$ 16

Since a tax law takes money from people, rather than paying money to them, what connection does the tax law have with the topsy-turvy welfare system in the news story? The connection lies in the way Congress has played fast and loose with the sixteenth Amendment to the Constitution, and with the principle of basing taxes on "ability to pay."

The sixteenth Amendment, which authorized the first United States income tax, empowered Congress to tax "incomes, from what*ever sources derived."* (Italics mine.) That expresses the Gertrude Stein-ish notion that a dollar is a dollar is a dollar and that, regardless of its source, the dollar endows its lucky recipient with 100 cents of

*Admittedly, the above "news story" sounds implausible, if not unbelievable. Yet the story is essentially true. The facts and figures in it are real. Such a system is, in fact, part of the law of the land. Only the law isn't called a welfare law. It goes by the name of "The Internal Revenue Code of 1954, as Amended"—the basic income-tax law of the United States.

"ability to pay" for food, shoes for the baby, a fraction of a yacht—or for taxes. Hence, in fairness, all dollars, no matter what their origin, should be taxed uniformly. But Congress has decreed differently. It has decreed that dollars earned in an oil or real-estate venture, in a stock market bonanza, or in interest on a state or local bond, while undeniably effective in buying food, shoes, or yachts, are somehow reduced in potency when it comes to paying taxes—for Congress has exempted such dollars, in whole or in part, from taxation.

The American tax system, which stipulates that rates rise as a person's affluence grows, also holds that a billionaire like oilman Jean Paul Getty—with a reported income of $300,000 a day—is better "able to pay" taxes than an impoverished Kentucky coal miner. In fact, under the tax rates supposedly applicable to all citizens, Mr. Getty's $100 million annual income endows him with an "ability to pay" about $70 million to the Internal Revenue Service (on the premise that he should be able to make do on the remaining $30 million each year). But since Mr. Getty's dollars come largely from oil ventures, they are not, by Congressional fiat, taxed like other dollars. In consequence, according to what President Kennedy told two United States Senators, Mr. Getty's income tax in the early sixties came nowhere near $70 million. It amounted to no more than a few thousand dollars—just about the amount a middle-income engineer or professor would pay.

Now compare the notion of excusing Jean Paul Getty from paying $70 million in taxes—taxes that an equally wealthy non-oilman would legally have to pay—with the notion that Mr. Getty is receiving a $70 million federal welfare check. In both cases the consequences are that:

Mr. Getty is $70 million richer.

The United States Treasury is $70 million poorer than if the full tax had been paid.

The rest of the taxpayers are obliged to pay an added $70 million to make up the difference.

Thus, the net effect of a "tax forgiveness" is identical to that of a direct federal handout.

The Brookings study concluded that of the $77.3 billion in tax "handouts," just $92 million gets to the six million poorest families in the nation, while twenty-four times that amount—$2.2 billion—is just the amount Congress voted last year for food stamps for 14.7 million hungry Americans. Moreover, five times that amount in the form

of "tax welfare" went to families earning more than $100,000 a year.

The disparity between the "tax welfare" for the wealthy and that granted the poor is even more breath-taking in the case of the "tax preferences" involving so-called "capital gains"—the profits on sales of stocks and bonds, land, buildings, and other kinds of property. When a person cashes in such profits during his lifetime, he pays no more than half the usual tax. Even more striking, all the gains in the value of property a person holds until death are not taxed at all. Some $10 billion entirely escapes taxation in that manner every year.

Since to have capital gains you have to own property (i.e., have the surplus cash to buy same), it's not surprising that only one taxpayer in twelve is able to report any gains, and that three quarters of such gains are enjoyed by the wealthiest 9 percent of America's taxpayers. Thus, all but the super-rich have a right to be envious, if not startled, by the Brookings figures on the "tax welfare" payments—the average per-family tax savings—granted capital gains recipients:

Yearly Income	Yearly "Tax Welfare" from Capital Gains
Over $1,000,000	$641,000
$500–1,000,000	$165,000
$100–500,000	$ 23,000
$20–25,000	$ 120
$5–10,000	$ 8
$3–5,000	$ 1

These federal handouts to the wealthy reach the astounding total of nearly $14 billion a year. But even that sum is dwarfed by the tax benefactions that Uncle Sam bestows on all but our poorest citizens the instant they are pronounced man and wife, a happy moment that carries with it the privilege of filing a joint return. The Brookings study reveals, startlingly, that the annual total of this giveaway to married couples comes to $21.5 billion.

Some, noting that the Environmental Protection Agency will only be permitted to spend one fourteenth that amount next year, have difficulty discerning how this $21.5 billion matrimonial "tax dole" benefits the national welfare. If it is supposed to be an incentive to marriage, it is a strange one indeed, since it shows a total indifference to the marital status of the poor, who derive no financial benefit from this tax giveaway whatever. Instead, it offers increasingly generous benefits the higher a couple's income goes, in brackets where it matters little whether two can indeed live as cheaply as one. Two thirds of this marital "tax welfare" goes to taxpayers making more than $20,000 a year, and less than 3 percent goes to the hardest-pressed married couples—those making less than $10,000 a year. These are the average per-family matrimonial tax savings:

Yearly Income	Yearly "Tax Welfare" to Married Couples
Under $3,000	$ 0.00
$3–5,000	$ 0.72
$5–10,000	$ 24.00
$25–50,000	$ 1,479.00
$100–500,000	$ 8,212.00
Over $1,000,000	$11,062.00

The basic question raised by the Brookings study is whether the unreviewed annual "tax welfare" of over $77 billion makes sense in a time of budgetary deficits averaging $30 billion a year, and in a time when we are plagued with "social deficits" (in housing, health, and the like) of vastly greater proportions. The Brookings experts propose an essentially preference-free, or "no-loophole," tax system. That would open up some choices that the present sievelike system forbids: it would make it possible to raise added revenues that could be applied to the nation's social needs. Or it could make possible a massive tax-rate reduction; Drs. Perchman and Okner say that in a no-loophole system, the present levels of federal revenues could be collected with tax rates ranging from 7 to 44 percent, instead of the present 14 to 70 percent. Or there could be a combination of both revenue-raising and rate-reduction. But whatever the choice, a preference-free system would put an end to irrational multibillion-dollar "tax expenditures" that continue to be perpetuated as long as Congress fails to act. It would also put an end to a tax system that is highly manipulable by the well-to-do (such as the 112 people with incomes over $200,000 who contrived to pay no tax whatever in 1970, despite the supposed Congressional effort in 1969 to stop such taxlessness), but that leaves largely helpless the vast majority of taxpayers whose taxes are withheld from their paychecks and whisked away before they even see the money.

What are the prospects for significant tax reform? On a strictly nose-count basis, the cause should be a popular one, especially when it comes to ending such preferences as capital gains (from which just one taxpayer in 12 benefits), or the multibillion-dollar tax favors to large corporations. But past loophole-closing efforts have provoked concentrated lobbying pressure on Congress while generating little public enthusiasm. So, as the Brookings study shows, the tax system is clearly not based on a popular nose count.

Some reformers, however, are beginning to tackle the problem in earnest. Fred Harris, a former Senator from Oklahoma and member of a People's Tax Action Campaign, is in hopes of creating a ground swell of popular support for a drastic revision of the tax system. President Nixon has his own formula for tax reform, and Wilbur Mills, chairman of the House Ways and Means Committee, plans to devote much attention to the issue. Even such diverse groups as Common Cause and the National Welfare Rights Organization give tax reform a high priority, and their enthusiasm has already resulted in a growing interest in the subject. If the momentum can be maintained, and the necessary coalitions interwoven, there exists the possibility that the 93rd Congress might be forced to radically curtail at least a portion of Uncle Sam's welfare program—for the rich.

> "Uncle Sam will not be the inspiration of the free world while the major cities of America are clogged with trash and pollution and taxpaid welfare loafers wallow in litter and debris."
> Senator Russell Long
> August 6, 1971

PURPOSE:
To prepare people for visiting a Senator to discuss tax reform.

ASSUMPTIONS:
Fairer taxation will not happen until people demand it.
People will demand it when they fully understand the present system and are assisted in learning how to change it.

PREPARATION:
Know how to help people understand the tax law.

TIME:
1 hour

MATERIALS:
Stern's article, "Uncle Sam's Welfare Program for the Rich"
How to Visit a Legislator
Two meeting rooms

PROCEDURE:

A. Beginning: *(5 minutes)*
  1. Begin session by reading opening "news" account in Stern article. It begins on page 89.
  2. Review discussion from last session.
  3. Announce that Senator Rich, who is one of the U.S. Senators from our state, happens to be in town and we are planning to visit him on the subject of tax reform. Ask for volunteers to play Senator Rich and his aide.

B. Small Groups: *(15 minutes)*
  1. We will need to get ready to present our views to him. Divide into random groups of three to prepare for the meeting. Groups should prepare arguments. One spokesperson should be selected from each group. Refer to Stern's criticism.

C. Visit: *(20 minutes)*
  1. Reassemble for visit to Senator Rich in a separate room. Note attached advice on how to visit a legislator.
  2. Group assembles, but Senator Rich sends legislative aide, who apologizes because the Senator was called away at the last moment.
  3. Presenters make their case to the legislative aide, who argues that:
  We are all better off with tax "incentives" going to those with the means to invest.
  The economy needs these incentives to stay healthy.
  Such incentives to the rich give the poor something to aspire toward.
  The wealthy, being better educated, can spend the money more wisely.
  Group signs Senator's guest book, is given a copy of his newsletter to his state, and is ushered out.

D. Discussion: *(15 minutes)*
  1. Return to first room and discuss the meeting. The Gas Meter used in Games Pharaohs Play would be useful here. *(5 minutes)*

E. Conclusion:
  1. Read aloud Amos 8:1-14.
  2. Ask members of the group to stand if they are willing to plan a real, live visit to their Senator or Representative within two months (next Congressional recess, when legislator is home). Begin planning this visit with those who stand.

SUPPORTIVE RESOURCES:
How to Visit a Legislator (page 134)
Gas Meter (page 115)

PURPOSE:

To help people begin to realize what power they have for change in society and how important it is to work as a group.

To help people appreciate the many possible actions that are not violent or corrupt.

ASSUMPTIONS:

People have more power than they think.

People are robbed of their power but they also willingly hand it over and even cooperate in their own oppression.

Religiously oriented people often assume that the only power in society is violence and corruption; but, in fact, there are many acts of power that are not violent or corrupt.

PREPARATION:

Arrange for someone to read the Sharp list of nonviolent action.

Plan dramatically to impress on people that there are at least 194 types of action available to them.

TIME:

1½ hours

MATERIALS:

Methods of Nonviolent Action, a list by Gene Sharp

Newsprint and markers or chalkboard and chalk

PROCEDURE:

A. Begin with a Brainstorming Session: *(25 minutes)*

 1. Ask people to name all the possible types of actions people can take to change things, such as voting, writing legislators, etc. List them on newsprint or chalkboard.

 2. When people run out of actions to list, ask them if there are any special types of action that Jesus' followers should concentrate on. List, if any.

 3. Let the whole thing peter out. Ask if they are sure that's all. Let the silence reign.

B. Dramatic Reading: *(15-20 minutes)*

 1. Then, as prearranged, a reader begins to read the list of Methods of Nonviolent Action by Sharp.

 2. Try to list them all, run out of space, get behind, ask for help. Then give up and let the list drone on.

C. Analyze an Action: *(1 hour)*

 1. Assign a problem to the whole group, such as: You all are renters in an apartment building for which you pay from $200 to $400 a month (adapt prices to the average rates in your area). You have just received notice from the landlord of a 30 percent increase in rent due to "increase in maintenance and security." What are you going to do about it? (The above is merely an example. You may want to choose another problem or issue closer to the participants' experience or interest.)

 2. Force Field Analysis: *(30 minutes)*

  a. Explain that people should list all the positive, enabling forces on their side related to their problem. Make a vertical list. Then list all the negative, constraining forces on a parallel vertical list.

  b. Then list all the actions that they can take to increase the positive forces and to decrease (or neutralize) the negative forces.

  c. Divide group into working groups of five and have them set priorities for their actions. Make the Sharp list available to them.

 3. In plenary session have each group of five report on its analysis and priorities. Compare the reports. Allow time for discussion.

D. In conclusion, read John 5:1-14, "Take up your pallet and walk."

SUPPORTIVE RESOURCES:

The Methods of Nonviolent Action (pages 135–37)

PURPOSE:
To simulate an action so people can learn what their power is and how to use it.

ASSUMPTIONS:
To know something well, one must do it. A simulation of doing it is second best to actually doing it. It is assumed that Part 1, What's to Be Done?, has been completed.

PREPARATION:
Coach the landlord and an assistant privately. (The landlord role card is a secret.)
Note that other issues could be substituted, such as a 30 percent utility hike, a cut in welfare, or a tax increase.
The question of rent is, however, a microcosm of others and is therefore especially useful.

TIME:
1 hour

MATERIALS:
Copies of Cardinal Rules for Making Change
Action plans from What's to Be Done?
Landlord Role card

PROCEDURE:

A. Beginning: *(10 minutes)*
   1. Assign roles, asking for volunteers to be landlord and assistant. Assign one group to act as renters; the rest should become critical bystanders.
   2. Get into roles. Ask renters to polish up their action approaches. The critical bystanders are given copies of the Cardinal Rules for Making Change and asked to study them in preparation for critically observing the renters' action. Coach the landlord in his or her role.
   3. Tell people that there is a winning combination.

B. Rent Action: *(20 minutes)*
Action follows in this order:
   1. Landlord and assistant are in separate rooms.
   2. Renters go to see landlord.
   3. Renters carry out actions and adapt them to landlord's responses.
   4. Each response should be planned and carried out until time is up.

C. Reflections: *(30 minutes)*
   1. Have critical bystanders comment according to Cardinal Rules. Have landlord respond to what influenced him or her. Have general reflection on the actions and responses and the way power operated.
   2. Brainstorm implications. Housing is a microcosm of many large community, national, and world problems. Ask how this experience applies to them.
   3. End with a reading of James 1:19-27, "Be doers of the word."

SUPPORTIVE RESOURCES:
Cardinal Rules for Making Change (page 138)

Landlord Role

1. You need some extra cash for new housing investment and prefer to up the rent rather than go to the bank. But you will seek a loan, if the renters are too upset. It's not too critical. It's just an issue of "what the market will bear."

2. You will settle for a 10 percent increase, no less, to keep up with your true costs.

3. You are no pushover; you believe renters should fight for what they get.

4. You give in only after a number of their tries and not then unless they find the winning combination, which is a combination of respect for your legitimate needs and the firm, determined pressure that makes it cost you more than it's worth to hold the 30 percent increase.

5. Use a number of tools and the Gas Meter. Begin with being out of town and sending your assistant to see them.

BACKGROUND READINGS ON USING POWER

1. SOCIAL-CONTROL MECHANISMS

This section further amplifies the third step in social change. When we become conscious of our social conditions and have developed clear visions and alternatives to them, it is time to take on the most basic aspect of intergroup behavior: power.

Power is the only currency one can spend in this large-group world. Little else matters. One can no more change society without using power than one can live with other people without love. Power is basic. You can't ignore it. However, power is a loaded word and a touchy subject. Let us make a few preliminary points before we proceed.

First, it is the peculiar nature of education for social change that the style of action depends on what issues are being dealt with. Different education and action programs are undertaken in different countries, in different economic groups, and in different age groups. One cannot use the same approach in organizing small farmers as is used with housing tenants. This limits how specific we can be regarding the application of the use of power. However, some important general points can be made, especially as regards church participation in the uses of power.

Second, social issues are immensely fluid; what is timely this spring has changed by next fall. This again limits some specific details, but not all.

Third, we are basically concerned here about morally motivated or, at least, church-related social change activity. Therefore, the distinction between the four types of power made on pages 46–47 should be kept in mind. If, as we affirmed there, the best choices for the church are the use of moral power and some forms of political power, we still need to distinguish a further point: the motivation for using power. In principle, the church's motivation for using power is distinct. For instance, we may find ourselves joining a strike against a company and walking in a picket line behind one person who simply wants more pay for less work. Beside us is an agent provocateur who works for the company and seeks to break up the union. All of us are doing the same thing at this moment (picketing), but each from a different motivation. The next day we all may be doing very different actions, each depending on our varied motivations.

Coalitions

The example of distinctive motivations illustrates a critical principle in all social action, the *coalition* principle. Coalitions are very helpful institutions that the church has been a long time in discovering. Coalitions are helpful because they allow people with different motivations to act on the same problem and often to solve the problem to everyone's satisfaction. This can be done even if the people disagree on everything else. Coalitions break up stalemates and enable positive movement. Members of a coalition simply keep their disagreements to a minimum and their unique motivations to themselves and go ahead and act.

Another helpful aspect of a coalition is that it encourages the respect for other people that is often lost in a helper-charity relationship. For example, a church decides to do something about hunger. As it studies the problem, it discovers the complex social/economic factors that place it in a winner role against a world of losers, those who hunger. Now this church can decide to play a helper role and take up a collection for the hungry or it can become an ally and begin building coalitions that seek to change the structures that lead to hunger.

In order to play an ally role rather than a helper role, people must discover their own needs and interests and make them into a common cause with the hungry victims or any other dispossessed group it seeks to support. This is not easy work, especially for affluent churches in the United States. But it is a very helpful, conceptual breakthrough in the whole idea of Christian mission. If we can become allies of and enter into coalitions with the hungry, the poor, and the oppressed, we can then avoid many of the problems that come with Band-Aid charity and dependency. Ideally, allies in coalition do not dominate or become dependent on one another. They are interdependent equals.

This coalition approach is highly recommended here as an appropriate way the church can use power in society and still maintain its unique integrity as a church.

As we discuss more specific ways the church can use power (that is, moral power and limited political power, as opposed to moralistic power and power politics), it is critical that we are "wise as serpents" about the tactics of power politics. Here we will define these tactics, or social-control mechanisms, after which we will discuss the appropriate areas of church use of power and conclude with a checklist of questions about power use.

The Tactics of Power Politics

Individual people have ways of fouling up their lives with gluttony, sloth, pride, and all those sinful things we seem to enjoy doing. Small groups of people also foul up relationships with deceptive games people play. Since it is one of the basic themes in this book that large groups also have their own ways of fouling up intergroup relationships, we will spell them out in some detail. These mechanisms of dominance and dependence are social sins in that they corrupt the structures of society and weaken the basic moral support and trust necessary for a society to hold together. Therefore, it is essential for socially active persons to be able quickly to detect these mechanisms. They all have in common the effort by the dominant group to keep power by making the decisions and rules and by the dependent group to cooperate in this arrangement by following the rules and decisions. It is a cooperative effort. The mechanisms below are linked together, dominant on the left and dependent on the right. These two groups are paired and then clustered into basic conditions, rewards, and punishments.

Dominant Perspective   Dependent Perspective

BASIC CONDITIONS

Slavery's Normal	That's Life
"Alcoholics can't change."	"We can't fight City Hall."

Slavery's Normal is the basic theme of the dominant group. The dependent group responds with a That's Life attitude. Both express the theological heresy of fatalism. As regards social reality, fatalism denies that the dominant group is accountable for (and that the dependent one is capable of) social responsibility. The fundamental theme of the Bible is *against* fatalism and is *for* a responsive and accountable relationship between people and people, and people and God. To be human is to be capable and accountable not only for self but for society.

Deciders Rule	Follow the Leader
"Don't worry, I'll handle those decisions for you.	"Go along to get along."

Deciders Rule (or Rulers Decide) is the dominant group's second article of faith. In response, the powerless play Follow the Leader. The powerless are fond of phrases like "I had no choice," "It's not up to me," "See the boss," "I couldn't help it." The dominant ruler fills in the power vacuum that this attitude creates. It's a vicious cycle because dominant groups also help create the follow the leader attitude. Rulers and followers cooperate with each other in these mechanisms.

REWARDS

For the folks who follow the leader and obey his/her rules, there are "rewards." These may be almost anything except two things: A dominant group will never give up the power to make decisions or the power to rule.

Protection	Obedience
"Protection racket"	"Love and obey till death . . ."

Protection is one reward. The dominant group has a stencil which it takes all around the country and paints "for your protection" on all kinds of structures, such as jails, hotel commodes, and TV scanning devices. Even outlaws from Al Capone to the SLA take hostages into "protective custody." The dependent group cooperates with this protection by obedience. They feel warm and cozy in it. And they collaborate, inform or get brainwashed, or turn "state's witness." Even the social institution of marriage traditionally calls on the man to love and "protect," the woman to love and "obey." Protection as such is not evil. Children, endangered species, and whole societies must be protected. The point is its misuse by power politics to increase dominance/dependence by denying the means of *self*-protection.

Pedestal	Flattery
"Ladies first."	"The boss smiled at me today."

Another "reward" for following and obeying is Pedestal. Pedestal provides no protection and, to be sure, no power, only honor. This is a curious kind of honor which makes no difference in the power balance and is top-down honor. It can readily be observed (1) in the custom where a "gentleman" says, "Ladies first," (2) in the honor politicians pay to dead soldiers and colleagues, (3) in the monuments erected to conquered people, and (4) most of all, in the empty honor often paid to Jesus on a pedestal. It is called "empty" honor because it risks nothing and gives the "honored" no power, no claim on one's life. Pedestal is easy to play and very effective in flattering people into thinking they are empowered when they are not. The dependent people cooperate in Pedestal by being flattered. Badges are worn, trophies collected, pictures taken, framed, and displayed. But it all happens *to* the powerless, as if by chance or magic. The boss dispenses compliments (verbal pedestals) sparingly and selectively. The powerless have the job of waiting and working for these symbols of appreciation. Again, these activities in themselves are personally gratifying and humanly satisfying but on a level of power politics they are often misused simply as a power play.

Steal Culture	Deny Identity
"The Cleveland Indians"	"I can't go home again."

Often a dominant group will "reward" a dependent minority by public displays of their culture—that is, the creative expressions of art, music, dance, folklore, and history of the dependent group. This can be valuable to the dependent group if they decide how it is used. But often the dominant group simply *steals the culture* of the dependent group and robs them of their art, music, dance, their folklore, history, even their names—their own unique identity. Slavery of Blacks accomplished much of this. More subtle cases include the use of Indians and their lore in scouting programs, the loss of women's names in marriage, the elimination of selected historical events in textbooks, the use of dependent people predominantly as entertainers, athlete/gladiators, jesters, and mascots.

The role of the powerless in this social-control mechanism of stealing culture is for them to *deny identity.* They are taught and they practice self-abuse by being embarrassed by their own culture, group, or class. It is repressed and made an object of shame, mockery, and rejection. Women often introduce themselves not only as Mrs. John Somebody but as "onlyahousewife." Blacks have stopped cooperating in the mechanism by growing rather than straightening their hair and casting off their slaveowner's names. Rubem Alves in *Tomorrow's Child* points out how the Jews in Babylonian captivity resisted the stealing of their culture by constantly renewing their identity and refusing to entertain their captors.

> By the waters of Babylon,
>   there we sat down and wept,
>   when we remembered Zion.
>   On the willows, there we hung up our lyres.
> For there our captors
>   required of us songs,
> and our tormentors, mirth, saying,
>   "Sing us one of the songs of Zion!"
> How shall we sing the Lord's song in a
>   foreign land?
>
> —Psalm 137:1-4

Cooptation	Privateer
"Join us and we'll see what we can do for you."	"When I'm rich, I'll help."

Dependent people are also "rewarded" by being selectively brought into some aspect of the dominant culture for the purpose of "buying off" their leadership or granting a little in order to keep much. Stealing culture is a form of cooptation. But cooptation also refers to the dominant group's swallowing up not only a minority's culture but its leadership, ideas, and programs. Tokenism is a form of cooptation in which dependent persons are given minor roles in the dominant society as a public relations effort. The dependent group always has individuals who cooperate for their own private advantage. This is called privateering. No personal guilt should be attached to this attempt to gain private advantage; often it's the only option for a person, and the problem is a social, not a personal, one, solvable only by changing the social structure.

It is a very common occurrence, however, for the most skilled persons to be consumed by a dominant society. This process is also called the brain drain, by which the best-educated persons in a poor nation or state come to study in a rich area and stay for their own advantage and to the disadvantage of their native area where they are needed most. This phenomenon is endemic to an unjust social condition. But power politics knows how to use it for its own benefit.

Enforce Decadence	Fleshpot
"Drugs flow in the ghetto."	"Eat bonbons and read novels."

We have mentioned in the Theological Survival Kit how a colonial power will corrupt its colonies with unhealthy drugs, alcoholism, and materialism, like the soma pills that docile people took in the book *Brave New World.* These are cases of enforced decadence which render dependent people more dependent. The role assumed by the recipients of these "rewards" is taken from the name that the Israelites gave to their comfortable slavery, "fleshpot." It's very common knowledge that materialism corrupts people and makes them fat, contented, and powerless, what the prophet Amos calls "cows of Bashan." What is not often acknowledged is that such decadence can, and is, used as a tool of power politics.

Bread and Circuses	Magic, Miracle, and Chance
"Chevrolet brings you the super Super Bowl."	"You too can be a lucky winner."

Dominant groups not only ask to be entertained by songs of Zion, they also offer the "reward" of entertainment. The phrase "bread and circuses" originated during the Roman Empire when soldiers began to mutiny. In response, the emperor gave them bread to eat and circuses to distract them. All kinds of distraction in a society can be used this way—sports, sensational and gossip journalism, song and dance—anything that is harmless to the dominant group and pacifying to the dependent group. Dependent people are taught to take the bread and circuses and to expect change to happen irrationally, if at all. Magic, miracle, and chance become the only sources of hope. Superstition, gambling, and all sorts of mumbo jumbo enchant them. They live stupefied by nonsense that keeps them incapable of solving their problems in rational and self-reliant ways.

Band-Aid	Thankyouthankyou
"Help the poor."	"Don't bite the hand that feeds you."

In a social, large-group context, treating symptoms rather than causes of social injustice not only helps little but often is harmful. Band-Aid is the bad name of charity in which ameliorative efforts simply reinforce the structured causes of problems and increase dominance and dependence. Examples of this are the paint-dobbing brigade to the ghettos, the charity ball of the rich, the token gestures of guilt money and labor given to oppressed people. Dependent people have little choice in this Band-Aid effort. Often they are so desperate that they must take gifts and help if they are to survive. The mistake they make is that of being overly grateful. This blinds them to the structures of injustice. By saying and thinking *Thankyouthankyou,* they cooperate in Band-Aiding a problem rather than attacking the cause.

PUNISHMENTS

The foregoing are some of the "rewards" the dominant group provides. They all constitute a one-way "gift," in that dependent people rarely choose them. This is the whole point, of course: to keep the decision and rule-making in control of the dominant. This is the game of power politics. Even arbitrary reward, however, has its own implied arbitrary punishment. If one group has the power to reward, they also have the power to punish. This they will do also, if punishing is required to maintain power.

Apartheid	Know My Place
"Redlining"	"I don't deserve better."
"Separate but equal"	"I know where I belong."

In order to be "rewarded and punished," a dependent group must be distinguished from the rest of society. Hitler distinguished Jews by requiring them to wear a Star of David on their clothing. This was one of the first steps in the separation and final annihilation of millions of Jews. In South Africa, the apartheid policy places Blacks in Bantustands. In the United States, Blacks go into ghettos and Indians go onto reservations. Women traditionally have been kept in the circumscribed areas of kitchen, child care, and church. We can simply call this apartheid. These types of separation from society are obvious. However, we need to ask how this basic social-control mechanism operates. What are the patterns and procedures it follows? Apartheid is the physical separation of a whole group of people defined in terms of their group identity rather than by any other human trait.

Segregation, discrimination, concentration camps are other examples of this physical separation. More subtle types of apartheid are based on educational and economic distinctions.

Except for racial segregation in the United States, we find it very hard to detect instances of segregation, much less apartheid—that is, types of physical separation based only on group identity. Of course, it is hard to see social-control mechanisms at work when we are born into them and accept them as natural. Like fish at sea, we do not think about the water we live in. And clearly we do not have a monarchical class or caste system as in Europe or India. However, we are segregated—that is, physically limited to certain areas of our society—on the basis of education and economics.

> Just by looking at the map of a city one can identify the zones of pain and those of comfort. Check the real estate section of a newspaper. The price of a house in the area you have your eye on will tell you whether it is a "nice neighborhood" or not . . . certain groups are destined to work more, suffer more, earn less, die sooner, and endure discrimination. Others work less, earn more, have more pleasure, have a better chance of living longer, and enjoy prestige and status.*

In general, apartheid limits one's physical access on the basis of one's group identity; this functions in a society apart from an individual's ability freely to choose otherwise. Very often the people who are segregated accept these boundary lines because they do not believe they deserve to have better. This is especially true among people who have less education or certain low-paying jobs. They don't have to be kicked out of exclusive clubs or schools. They know their place. They remain in their ghettos, "with their own people," voluntarily. Dependent people have barbed wire in their brains which tells them automatically that places beyond their ghetto are off limits. Most social controls don't need police forces; they are obeyed because of the internal police which we are conditioned to fear. Apartheid is a given social condition, but, like all social mechanisms, it is changeable.

_____
*Rubem Alves, *Tomorrow's Child* (New York: Harper & Row, 1972), p. 112.

Limit Access	Play Dumb
"We would hire them, but they are not qualified."	"I'm afraid to try."
	"I can't, I'm too dumb."
"Better pay—better homes—better schools—better jobs and vice versa."	

One of the reasons dependent people are sometimes less efficient in carrying out work or other social roles is that they have had their horizons confined to their segregated schools and limited jobs. They have fewer opportunities to explore various options or even to begin to practice normal first class citizenship.

Dependent people are given the old mushroom treatment: Feed them plenty of fertilizer and keep them in the dark. In the dark, people are dependent on whoever has a match, so match owners are quick to exploit their advantages. They will show off their lights, sell them, build fires, but never give others the tools, skills, secrets—that is, access to making the matches. By monopolizing access to tools and materials that a dependent group is dependent on, a monopolizer can exercise enormous power. Monopoly sets its own price.

American Indians were conquered in a much more subtle fashion than by military defeat. They became dependent on white man's guns and lost the ability to survive without them. Depending on guns made Indians vulnerable to the white man who controlled the access to guns. Controlling and limiting access to vital knowledge and resources is a critical tool to power politics. The dependent group is called on to "play dumb." Their role is to be ready any time access is opened to them with an answer such as "I can't," "I'm too old," or "You do it; you're smarter." Play Dumb is an ingrained response to limited access. It's what most of us do when we are not skilled in certain areas. The problem develops when this mechanism is used deliberately to dominate a group of people.

Stereotype	Introjection
"Country bumpkin"	"Women drivers"
"Hard hat"	"Jew him down"

When the pharaoh wanted to explain the Hebrews' unrest in the brickyards of Egypt, he said they were idle or lazy and therefore tried to solve the problem by increasing their work load. Stereotypes exaggerate a common human trait and project it onto a whole group of people. It is normal to be lazy sometimes, to be emotional, to be thrifty, to be unlucky. But if you are a minority group and dependent on a majority culture, stereotype is a normal daily burden you have to bear. Stereotype publicizes one trait as characteristic of an entire people, but in this case it is not peculiar to that group, as the group's identity is. Rather, it is a universal human feature, like sexual desire, emotion, human error, or body odor.

Dependent people are often stereotyped as overly concerned with sex, as having less sexual discipline relative to the dominant mores. They are branded as sex-minded. But who isn't? "Women are emotional." So? Who isn't? "Youth are apathetic this year." That really doesn't communicate very much. Dependent people cooperate with this procedure by internalizing these stereotypes. They introject the false image and then sometimes carry it out.

These kinds of stereotypes are easy to detect, and few people use them with impunity in polite society. Less obvious are the ways we group people by their economic, job, educational, or residential status. People from certain schools are expected to act in predictable ways. People from the inner city find loans harder to get. Low-paying jobs also reduce one's credit rating. A person becomes identified by his or her work, so that one *is* a housewife, doctor, carpenter, or student rather than being a person who *does* these activities. Such economic stereotyping may give one momentary role security by job identity, but it distorts and stunts people's growth and full humanity and can become a tool for social control. As a social-control mechanism, stereotyping sorts people into desirables and undesirables, into job and age categories which lock them into socially controlled boundaries. The brand of "troublemaker," "radical," or "extremist" often stereotypes a person, so that he or she loses political effectiveness, even though most great people, especially religious heroes, were so named.

We all know better than to "kick a person while he or she is down." All but the worst social deviates are taught to help, not hurt, the weak, sick, young, and old who can't protect themselves

Blame the Victim	Blame Self
"Those people are asking for trouble."	"I'm as guilty as the next person."
"People on welfare are cheats."	"Guess I'm just inadequate."

well. And only a pathologically ill person would deliberately harm an already sick or victimized person. On an interpersonal level, it happens only as an exception to the rule. But that is on the interpersonal level. In intergroup relations, blaming or taking advantage of a weak person is the rule, not the exception. The logic of the large-group power machine functions differently. What is pathological behavior for individuals and small groups of people is a tool of power for power politics vis-à-vis large groups.

If power is the goal, then blaming and punishing weak people is a simpler, and easier, and more convenient way to gain power. Its goal is to win and control. That's all. So if a woman gets raped, a person on welfare is given only a 70 percent check, a convict is killed in prison, a worker loses a job, or the Hebrew slaves are beaten for not making enough bricks in Egypt, the pharaohs through the ages answer the same way to cries for mercy: "It's your own fault" and "You're lazy" (see Exodus 5:16-17).

This type of thinking and the human misery that results from it is another one of the problems caused by confusing two levels of thinking, the individual and the large group. There is much truth in the maxim, "You made your bed, you lie in it," at least on a personal level. That is, a person is required to live with, or lie in, the consequences of the deeds he or she freely decides to commit. But on a large-group level, Blame the Victim makes a whole group of people lie in the bed that someone else made. Both individuals and groups of dependent people as a whole have to pay the consequences for other people's decisions. Dependent people also blame the victim even when *they* are the victim. They blame themselves unless they begin to stand up to dominance and refuse to cooperate.

Pit the Victims	Fight Each Other
"Amnesty is not possible because loyal soldiers did their duty."	"Workers and environmentalists clash over plant construction."

Pharaoh's battle with Moses includes a classic case of Pit the Victims. He got the foremen and the taskmasters in the brickyards to fight each other. They were both victims of the oppression, but they fought among themselves. "Divide and conquer" was a textbook rule for colonial powers, and we all know how employees or students compete with each other to increase production or up the college board averages. Competition is a milder form of pitting the victims, but the principle is the same. Mass media news is forever looking for fights to report, especially among leaders of a dependent people. It is a popular tool of all tyrants, and victims cooperate by *fighting each other.*

Tighten the Screw	Gratitude for Small Favors
"Up the ante."	"Glad to be alive."
"Increase the work load."	"No raise is better than no job."

When the President of the United States decided to increase the bombing of North Vietnam, his purpose was to induce their surrender by, as he said, "tightening the screw." When Pharaoh wanted to calm down the slaves in the brickyard, he stopped giving them straw but demanded the same quota of bricks. He tightened the screw. This sometimes has the "ratchet effect" of "upping the ante" so that loosening the screw is received gratefully by those oppressed. The logic is one of increasing the pain, so that its release is accepted as good even though it's not better than before the screw was tightened. The verbal parallel to this approach is "So you think *this* is bad . . ." It's intended to induce gratitude for small favors. Pouty children often are controlled this way. Cleaning their room is not attractive until they must do it rather than clean the bathroom also. When the pain is increased, the ending of any of it is welcomed.

Zap	Vanish
"Benign neglect"	"Lie low till it passes."
"Selective silence"	"Shut up before you get us all in trouble."

Zap suggests a futuristic ray gun that causes unwanted people to disappear without a trace. In a social structure, large groups of people are ignored in a manner which simply abolishes all their influence, even the minimal influence of physical presence. Many people are not counted in census figures, especially minority persons and illegal immigrants. Benign neglect can become an official policy in which a group is simply ignored. Oppressed people become invisible in a society, like servants at a dinner; they are present but their presence makes no difference in the conversation.

The dependent group often cooperates by disappearing voluntarily. Afraid and unaware of the consequences of becoming visible, the dependent group often keeps quiet and prefers to remain anonymous.

Below is a summary list of the tactics of power politics just discussed:

Social-Control Mechanisms of Dominant/Dependent Social Group Otherwise Known as Social Sins or the Tactics of Power Politics

Dominant Perspective	Dependent Perspective
Basic Conditions	
1. Slavery's Normal	That's Life
2. Deciders Rule	Follow the Leader
Rewards	
1. Protection	Obedience
2. Pedestal	Flattery
3. Steal Culture	Deny Identity
4. Cooptation	Privateer
5. Enforce Decadence	Fleshpot
6. Bread and Circuses	Magic, Miracle, and Chance
7. Band-Aid	Thankyouthankyou
Punishments	
1. Apartheid	Know My Place
2. Limit Access	Play Dumb
3. Stereotype	Introjection
4. Blame the Victim	Blame Self
5. Pit the Victims	Fight Each Other
6. Tighten the Screw	Gratitude for Small Favors
7. Zap	Vanish

Politics/Power

These tactics of power politics are so prevalent that we are often discouraged from attempting to use any kind of power at all, or we fall into moralistic power, which pretends to be above the use of power. However, no one can escape the use of power. Like racing cars which have no clutch, we cannot find a neutral ground on an idle gear. Even our sanctuaries are not sanctuaries from tax benefits and political significance. The only issue is: What kind of politics, what kind of power, will we use?

The answer we gave on page 48 was that the church has two appropriate kinds of power to use, moral power and political power, as distinct from moralistic power and power politics. The following essay will briefly examine these two appropriate areas of church activity in society and the exploration of the church from inside.

2. THE CHURCH AND THE USE OF POWER

Appropriate Areas of Church Activity in Society

It is critical for persons working from a church base to know the areas of appropriate and inappropriate uses of power. If we are clear about those boundaries we can avoid many hassles. When we are doing the same activity (letter-writing, protest meeting, or leaflet-passing) as other people in a coalition, it is important to be very clear about our church-based motives. For example, when visiting Congress in Washington, D.C., we church people almost always have to explain our motives to Congressional people. The initial assumption they make about church people is that we are there to lobby for prayer in public schools or more special tax breaks for churches or other special church interests. We have to tell them that's not our motive. We are not pleading especially for the church's benefit but for those without a voice, those who are powerless. In terms Congress can understand, our motives are for the "public interest" rather than "special interest." In our terms, our moral mandate is not to seek to build up our own church's power, but to seek a power transfer from the dominant to the dependent group toward the distant goal of interdependence. This includes the use of moral power and political power. So "public interest" is closer to our motivation than special interest. "Public interest" lobbying is simply one form of the use of political power such as that exercised by Common Cause and other public-interest groups.

The two areas of appropriate church use of power are political power and moral power. Moralistic power and power politics are inappropriate uses for the church because if we fall into these we lose our credibility and our integrity as a church. The church has its own history, motives, and unique self-identity. If we engage in power politics, we rightly lose that identity and integrity and become just one power group among others. If we engage in the use of moralistic power, we are seeking our own special interest and seeking to impose our own religious establishment on others by means of political power, although all kinds of pious gobbledygook may be used to deny and fog up this reality.

If we know our limits in the use of political power and moral power, then we can quickly answer those who charge us with special-interest lobbying or with becoming church politicians. Our mandate as a church is to be the voice of moral power in society. That is our first and nonnegotiable position. However, when it is possible in any particular society, we can appropriately engage in the use of political power within limits. In the Western countries those limits are set more or less within a basic division of church and state and within the tax codes. In the United States, if churches want to maintain their tax exemption, they must never campaign for a political candidate for public office or lobby for legislation to a "significant" degree. ("Significant" is roughly defined as 5 percent of the church agency's budget.)

Let's sort this out further. The church's integrity as church always requires it to assert moral power: to witness to its faith. This seems harmless enough to most countries, so it is usually permitted, even in the Soviet Union and Central Europe, although this witnessing is often confined to homes and church buildings. In Jesus' time during the Roman occupation, political power was not possible for him to use, but moral power was. Paul as a Roman citizen could get involved somewhat more in political power, as he used his claim to citizenship to express his Christian teaching. In the Middle Ages these distinctions became blurred when the church assumed some of the functions of the state.

Now in countries where voluntary associations are permitted a public voice and where church and state are separate, as in the United States and Canada, political power is available to the church in a limited way. Moral power is not limited by the state. But the church can never again assume major political power, or engage in power politics, without losing its separate identity as the institution with moral credibility and thus moral power. To lose moral power is to become impotent. Moral power is the church's basic calling, one it can continue even during times of totalitarian regimes.

The worst dictators have not been able to destroy the church's moral witness, not in Rome, in Russia, or in Nazi Germany. Although no political power may be available in these bad times, in good times, the church comes out from underground and broadcasts its moral power and gets involved in political powers in limited ways. But always it needs to be certain to distinguish itself from the state and to guard against the temptations of using corrupting power politics and the special pleading of moralistic power.

Appropriate Areas of Activity Within the Church

We have defined the areas of church use of power in society, but how do we get it moving within the church itself? Where do we begin Christian education for social change and how do we keep it going? A look at the general types of functions within the church will help guide us. Most of the actual life of churches can, I believe, be placed in four basic categories: liturgy, community, education, and outreach. Finance and building are large items in a church's life, but they are secondary functions which intend to make these other functions possible.

By liturgy, we are referring to all symbolic acts, celebrations, worship services, blessings, prayers, and ritual. Community includes all meetings or parts of meetings of people for the purpose of or the result of building interpersonal relationships, such as fellowships, couples clubs, coffee and tea hours, dinners. Education refers to all active learning, formal and informal, planned and unplanned. Outreach has two basic types: word and deed. Both extend beyond the church itself as mission to or with others. In practice, all these functions intertwine and often go on at the same time. Sermons can be educational. Outreach can be community building and can include liturgy. But these four categories seem to define four separate functions in the church.

Now we can return to the task of untangling the individual, small-group, and large-group approaches which focus our church activity within the church. It seems especially helpful to distinguish what we are trying to do in liturgy, community, education, and outreach if we are clear about which group we are seeking to impact. Liturgy that is intended for the inspiration of individuals is different from that liturgy intended for building groups, outreach that intends to end hunger will fail if it seeks only to feed individual stomachs.

So let us apply our groupings to church life itself for the purpose of defining the best places to work for education for social change.

1. *Liturgy* has many purposes, which are all summed up in religious terms like "word" and "sacrament" and "proclaiming the gospel." But can we identify any overall result (though it is an unmeasurable result) that we expect as we lead or participate in any service? Yes, this is possible. In our country church liturgy traditionally has sought the result of personal inspiration—that is, to lift up individuals with the good news.

Only in more recent times, in what Paulo Freire calls the "modern church," have we sought deliberately to inspire interpersonal communion. We do this by means of dialogue sermons, feedback sessions, the kiss of peace, more informal presentations, discussions, and singing. "Building community" during worship has become an important focus. The valuable discoveries of human growth training and other aspects of group dynamics learning have been integrated into liturgy or, as they are now called, "celebrations." Personal inspiration is intended here also, to be sure, but in a larger context of interpersonal inspiration.

A subtle but important difference can be made in liturgy which functions with an intergroup consciousness. Not only are individual and interpersonal inspiration sought but in addition (in what Freire calls the "prophetic church") liturgy includes an aspect of social concern beyond the church. Solidarity or group *oneness* within the church is sought. By oneness we do not mean interpersonal community as such but oneness in a vision beyond itself—that is, a sense that we here in this sanctuary are a socially significant and socially accountable group who can do something in the world. This intergroup aspect is a corporate consciousness about socially defined issues.

All three aspects of personal and interpersonal inspiration as well as group oneness are vital to liturgical acts within the church. Christian education for social change has a very important role in keeping the function of building group oneness alive in liturgy.

2. *Community* activity in the church goes on unintentionally in liturgy and all over the church. It is also done intentionally in certain times and places and with a certain focus.

We can build community with the basic intention of supporting individuals. We can build community with the basic intention of making acquaintances and sensitizing people to work effectively in small groups. And we can build community with the basic intention of organizing a group for effective education and action. Education for social change will, of course, stress the organizing or corporate-action aspect of community. But the neglect or belittling of support and group sensitizing will undermine the corporate mission.

All of these are important aspects of community building, but they require different skills and different results are expected. Supporting, sensitizing, and organizing are three types of community building that fit into the individual, interpersonal and intergroup categories respectively or, to use Freire's terms, the "traditional," "the modern," and the "prophetic" church.

3. *Education* also functions on three levels or groups. Each has its own distinct features. The traditional, individual-centered church education focuses on learning and knowing the word as it comes to us from the past. Interpersonal education in the modern church focuses on experiencing and relating and being the word in the present. The intergroup focus of the "prophetic" church focuses on action and reflection in the future. These often overlap; but knowing, being, doing tend to be the focus of these three approaches, with the expected results of: (1) moral individuals, (2) good group process, (3) group performance. Education for social change seeks all three results but emphasizes the group's performance in action and reflection.

4. The *outreach* function of the church is done with words and deeds. The church program that concentrates on reaching out to individuals alone on a one-to-one (each one teach one) basis will seek personal salvation of individuals by proclaiming the Word and will seek to help individuals. This is obvious enough, but it is distinct from the interpersonal and intergroup approach. The small-group approach tends to reach out with the word of invitation to join a small group in which love and support occur. Deeds are deeds of personal growth, not only by means of the individual conscience or personal prayer and Bible study but by means of interpersonal dynamics.

The intergroup approach reaches out by proclaiming the word of salvation by liberation. Liberation, like salvation, cannot be given from one person or group to another. Liberation is both a gift of God and a task for the people. Freire observes that oppressed people live in "silence." They speak words but they speak the words of the oppressor. The word of liberation requires that the oppressed find their own words and name their own world. The good news for large groups is the word of hope and the words of group esteem. "We are somebody and we have our own words, writings, culture, and a God who loves us too." Examples of people finding their own words can be noted in the slang, accents, and the subcultural styles and customs of people who are rising out of a culture of silence. Even church hymns and spirituals were used as a secret code of communication for Blacks in the days of slavery. A people's words define their world, and they have a right to name themselves and their world. The outreach of the prophetic church seeks to listen and to evoke the Word from the people rather than preach to them. This has profound implications for how we proclaim the good news in the future.

The outreaching deed deliberately limits its attempts to "help" and "invite." The large-group approach to deeds is an effort to change the conditions that make help necessary. The invitations are not to join our small group but to organize your own so that you are liberated from dependency.

Family of People

Education for social change does not so much seek to help or to preach to the "needy." We have finally learned that this approach assumes that we helpers and givers are superior to the needy. Rather, we all (rich and poor, oppressed and oppressor, dominant and dependent) are in it together as God's children. As we all find our own weaknesses and needs as groups of people, we can become allies with the oppressed. We can build coalitions around our common visions and common tasks.

This notion of allies in coalition fits well with the basic biblical metaphor of human relations. The Bible does not distinguish individuals, small groups, and large groups as we have done. Rather, the most persistent metaphor of human grouping is the family. If seen from the perspective of intergroup social consciousness, the biblical metaphor of family with a single parent (God) must replace the prevailing metaphor of state of siege. As the church works in society and builds allies and coalitions of equals, it must keep in mind the final vision: a human family of sisters and brothers living in justice and peace.

The moral imperative for the church is no longer a private "self-realization," to "become actually what one is essentially," as Paul Tillich said. The moral imperative is for humanity to become brothers and sisters in a family of people. The moral imperative is not merely internal personal growth or growth in groups. It is global growth toward self-chosen interdependence where dominance and dependence are abolished. This growth has to do with practical things that families do: providing food, shelter, energy, hope, meaning, and free decision-making. The moral has become the practical.

Christian Education for Social Change
Within the Church
The Objective of Each Church Function According
to Group Size

Church Function	Individual	Interpersonal	Intergroup
Liturgy	Personal inspiration	Interpersonal communication	Group oneness or solidarity
Community	Support of individuals	Make acquaintances Sensitize people in small groups	Organize
Education	Learning } the Knowing } past	Experiencing } in the Relating } present	Action } on the Reflec- } future tion
Outreach Word	To save —personal salvation	To grow —invitation to join	To liberate —name our world
Deed	—help individuals	—interpersonal growth	—change the conditions

3. QUESTIONS OF POWER: A CHECKLIST

As we seek our vision of a good world, it is useful to discipline ourselves with a simple, easy-to-recall checklist of questions so we can keep ourselves heading in the direction of that vision. There are many disciplines involved in using power to obtain our vision, but the simplest are the three questions; *What* are you doing? *Who* is doing it? *When* will it get done?

1. What

What are you doing and what results do you expect? This question must constantly be asked. The answer is a particular part of the larger vision one has for society. No one can stuff envelopes for very long unless there is a greater vision toward which this job is headed: "a fair deal," "new deal," "better deal," "big deal" that is some answer to

what it's all for and about. That's the big vision, but there are many steps back from this vision, which includes a five-year plan, a one-year plan, and getting all those stamps licked by this afternoon. What it is you are seeking determines how you use power.

What results do you expect? Do you want to expose the issue to build awareness? Do you expect to analyze the issue to inform others? Do you expect to involve people in particular actions? Do you expect these actions to serve those in need or to change the conditions that cause the need? Do you expect to witness to your convictions and/or call others to reflection and a reexamination of their own convictions? All of these (awareness, analysis, action, and reflection—AAAR) are important, but it is essential to know clearly and exactly what results you expect. If you fail to obtain those results, you will know to change your act next time. If you succeed, you will know you have succeeded and you can celebrate.

2. Who

Who has power and who uses power is easy to determine. This is one of our basic theses. The folks who make the decisions and the rules are the people with the power. This is clear in theory but very foggy in reality. It is not only hard to see through a barrage of rhetoric whom to hold accountable for something, but it's hard to communicate to others that the "up front" people are often only image makers for those folk in the back room. So here are some concrete cases or situations you can tear out and use to help communicate who has power.

CASE A:

Sara Minken, a twelve-year-old girl, announces at the family dinner table that she wants a minibike. The immediate laughter this evokes is followed by silence and then verbal efforts to define the issue. The issue is, Will she have the power to fulfill this want? Whoever decides that she will or will not have it and carries out the rules and arrangements for its purchase and maintenance will wield the power. That person will wield the power because his or her decision and rule making will serve as the capacity or ability to do, act, and change the present no-minibike arrangement.

Whose decisions and rules will prevail? (Take a minute here to think what you would do as a parent.) The traditional family order would leave the decision and ruling to the father, Ed Minken. Ed might say in an authoritarian way: "Shut up, Sara, and eat your chicken." Since, however, it turns out there are so many twelve-year-olds riding minibikes in the larger society, we can infer that the traditional parent rules in our society do not always prevail and that, in fact, some parents give in and say "OK." A permissive order may prevail; Ed can say "yes." Or Ed can avoid the decision. If he avoids it he may not be able to withstand those of Sara's power plays such as temper tantrums or pouting, that may accompany indecision or a "no" decision by Ed. If not, then Sara has learned a tool of power by which her decisions get implemented. Also, the dominant-parent/dependent-child relationship is reversed in this case; the parent becomes dependent upon the child's emotional moods. Who will decide and rule? Is it a win/lose battle? How can both win? How can both Ed and Sara make the decision together?

A shared decision-making situation may go like this; Sara does not have the experience and, in most cases, the money to get the machine. Ed's job as parent is to help Sara understand the requirements and consequences of these decisions and help Sara make a wise decision, along with him, which fully accounts for these requirements and consequences before and after the decisions are made. If this is done, Sara will need to assume the burden of purchase, ownership, maintenance, safety, noise, etc. Such a burden may cause Sara to change her mind. In any case, the burdens of ownership become real and are balanced with the desires of ownership. These are requirements and consequences that Ed Minken did not choose. They come with ownership of any machine. Therefore, Ed does not have to be held guilty or to blame for these natural requirements or consequences. If Sara groans, throws fits, or shows other signs of hatred for her father for mentioning these things, Ed can ignore them. He is not responsible for the requirements or the consequences. He, therefore, does not have to assume a dominating or dependent position. Neither does Sara have to take the role of total dependency. The power in this case is shared, interdependently. The goal is an interdependent decision-making process which shares power, in contrast to that of dependent powerlessness or of dominant power monopoly. The crucial point is: Whoever makes decisions and rules controls the power. The ideal for both Ed and Sara is to share the power by making the decisions and rules together.

CASE B:

A recent U.S. President was found to have used vast amounts of public money to improve his private estates. However, rather than repay the money, he decided to promise to give one of these estates to the public upon his death and the death of his wife. Many people thought this was a generous act. What exactly is wrong here? (Take a minute to state what's going on.)

This case illustrates that the ruler reserved for himself the decision about the use of his improved estate until he and his wife die. Rulers will give up anything, when forced to give up, except their decision-making capability. The reason is that power rests in decision making.

In contrast, the dependent person will do almost anything to avoid having to decide something. Daisy Buchanan in *The Great Gatsby* simply could not decide whom she loved most.

CASE C:

A mayor of Philadelphia, a staunch advocate of cutting public expenses, managed to get large salary increases for himself and the city council, the highest in the nation. His answer to criticism was that he would not collect his salary increase until retirement. What exactly is wrong here? (Take a minute to state what's going on.)

He would keep the decision-making power even if the salary increase were delayed.

CASE D:

You are in a doctor's office waiting to have your lungs examined for possible emphysema. The person waiting next to you lights up a cigarette. You say, "Pardon me, but do you have to smoke?" He says, "No, but I want to. I'm very nervous about seeing doctors." You say, "Yes, but that smoke is making me sick. Anyway, I believe I have a right to breathe fresh air." He says, "Tough luck, fellow. I have a right to breathe smoke." So the smoker's decision seems to rule. Why? What exactly is wrong here? (Take a minute to state what's going on.)

What is wrong is that he is imposing his decision on you, which is a decision to alter the natural, given condition of the air. If your decision to extinguish his cigarette and enjoy your right of fresh air were to rule, then he would not be equally imposed upon. Nonsmokers in natural, normal situations have a natural right. Smokers decide their historical (as opposed to natural) "right" to alter this condition. So the burden of the air pollution is on him because he could change it. You can't. If all this does not convince him, then offer to put your shoes back on if he will likewise contain his burnt odors.

CASE E:

We were at a conference in a lush building designed by Frank Lloyd Wright. Our group was given a tour of the beautiful architecture, art objects, and furniture. We all gawked at them and felt grateful that a big company foundation, Johnson Wax, had allowed us to enjoy the building. What exactly is wrong here? (Take a minute to state what's going on.)

A better knowledge of power would have tempered our gratitude. By forming a foundation, a practice legally and widely used by large companies and rich individuals, certain taxes on their profits did not have to be paid. Instead, this would-be tax money was placed in the foundation, to be used by the owners for some cause for which they decided to use it. Again, decision-making power remains in the hands of the rich. The taxes are not paid by them. Consequently, other people paid those unpaid taxes. Those same extra tax-paying people did not get mad about the extra tax burden they had to bear, but on the contrary, they gratefully appreciated the chance to see the fine art and architecture that Mr. Johnson had bought and to enjoy the accommodations the Johnson Foundation had decided to provide. My group did not yet understand how power works. Mr. Johnson did.

Who has power? is our question. The people who make the decisions and set the rules, and thus have power, are often not the people we initially think they are. The people who make public contact are only the press secretaries and public relations people. Even presidents of organizations can be mere figureheads. The sales clerks and service personnel whom we get mad at for bad products and services are rarely responsible. We have to look beyond the public image to the real decision makers. Even then we rarely will ever find the real person we are looking for. Chances are that the buck will stop at some desk where a very pleasant person (or group of people) sits. This person is a child of God also and as such deserves our respect as an individual. But this does not change the issue. We respectfully present our case. If he or she denies responsibility, we either move up the ladder or keep pressing here. The point is to find out who makes policy decisions and sets the rules that are causing the problem. On this stage, this person or persons are the antagonists, the adversary. For church people it should be clear that we are not talking about *personal* enemies. We never seek *personal* harm or even *personal* ill feelings. But like a drama (to be sure, a heavy drama), certain God-fearing people and others take on roles that are opposite from our roles. They are our *social* adversaries, not personal enemies. "Love your enemy," as Jesus says, but firmly, honestly, confront them with your position and don't let go.

Besides the antagonists are the protagonists, the *actors,* the doers, the players who are most interested in the change being sought. In every social situation this group is much smaller than the crowds they gather. In the jargon of social action, these are the "core," the "cadre," or the "change agents." They do the work.

The "constituency" is also vested in the issue but does not do much work besides maintaining membership, giving money, attending meetings, and voting. This is the group from which the actors are constantly being sought. Social action people spend many hours clearly defining who the constituency really is. Like the adversary, the people who are really touched by an issue are often different from first appearance. And the people who will even join as members are a more precise group still. Finding this out requires extensive research. This is called "defining the constituency."

Who is involved also includes the neutral people. These folks may be on one side or the other initially, but the role they play in the issue is neutral. Sometimes they can break a deadlock or negotiate a truce, but they basically remain aloof. Often actors seek to conscript the "neutrals" into

the "core"; failing that, they try to get them into the constituency; failing that, they are happy to see the neutrals remain neutral. It's better than their becoming adversaries.

3. When
The question of when a particular social change is to take place has three aspects. The answer to the question *when* separates the rhetoric from the commitment. Also, it helps bring a discipline to the matter of timing. But most important, when the actor expects the change to take place in great part determines the type of power to be used.

RHETORIC TO ACCOUNTABILITY
The best laid plans are just so much hot air until a date is set. This applies on a personal level in courtship and marriage but especially on a social change level, where politicians and other people of power know and use the tactic of "buying time." One effort in the peace movement to end the U.S. involvement in the Vietnam War was a three-year campaign to "set the date." It became necessary to focus an enormous array of demands to stop bombing, bring the troops home, end the draft, release political prisoners, negotiate now, etc., into one campaign push, an answer to the question *when*. It was a demand for a simple date for concluding our participating in the war, which had been promised for years. This campaign helped force Congress finally to vote a termination of military action in all of Indochina.

A date by which something must happen makes people accountable for their behavior and gives people seeking change a clear-cut tool for getting their demands met. If the commitment is not met, then the accountable party must suffer the charge of having reneged. This means a loss of credibility that he or she will seek to avoid.

TIMING
Timing is always central to change actions, but especially for Christians who separate *chronos* from *kairos*. *Chronos* is calendar time and *kairos,* as Paul Tillich has pointed out, is timing, the pregnant moment for action. *Kairos* is the "right time" to do something when "the times are ripe" for it. How does one know this? Besides revelations and prophecies, one must be wise and figure all the ingredients in an action/reaction to test the "timing and the times." Saul Alinsky illustrates this with the experience of the Chicago Woodlawn

Association's "move-in" on City Hall with demands about education. In preparing the action, they figured that they could get 8,000 people out but only for a limited time, after which the people would drift off to sightseeing and other distractions and the mayor would just sit tight and watch the crowd dwindle. So they made their demands at the right time, when 8,000 or so were present, and then said they were calling off the demonstration but would be back with the same number or more. "And with that they turned around and led their still enthusiastic army in an organized, fully armed, powerful withdrawal, and left this mass impression upon City Hall authorities."*

SHORT- OR LONG-TERM VICTORIES

The *when* (or time) to expect results is critical. When, in the vision, do you expect things to fall into place? A number of writers who have dealt with global, ecological, and energy issues have begun to recognize what theologians have always maintained. That is, as Barbara Ward said a few years ago, "At last, in the age of ultimate scientific discovery, our facts and our morals have come together to tell us how to live."† More recently, in a meeting of the World Future Society, Hazel Henderson, Co-director of the Princeton Center for Alternative Futures, said:

> Indeed we are now learning that self-interest, if seen in a large enough time/space context, is now *identical* with group interest, societal interest and species-interest. . . . For we now know that for the first time in our history, the teachings of all our great spiritual leaders (who have been real futurists): The Golden Rule, the edict to serve the people, the values of love, caring, sharing and tolerance-morality, in fact, has now become practical.‡

Facts and morals and practicality all come together eventually. The moral good is not only an abstraction, it is simply the longer-term benefit to a broader range of people than the short-term benefit to my group or your group. As we ask the *when* question about the use of power, we must from the religious/moral perspective ask after the long-term good for all people. They are the same

thing. Of course, being limited in our foresight, we cannot see what will definitely benefit most. But we can get some general outlines and visions if we, with study, prayer, and the gift of grace, are able to transcend our time and place even partially.

Faith, Love, and Hope

The Christian church for all its weakness always has this opportunity (indeed, this is its call) to transcend national and parochial limits and to use its strength of corporate moral action in society. The church is one of the very few social institutions with the specific purpose of moral action. The wistful expectation that good individuals or small groups alone can make a real difference in society has proven illusory. But the church is an organized body of people with great power if it chooses to use it.

If it does not seek social peace and justice, then other forces in society seeking their special interests will dominate. In order to move into the moral use of power, three spiritual values are necessary; faith, love, and hope. Individual faith establishes our personal commitment to give our lives as disciples of Jesus. Love brings us together with other people in close supporting communities. But hope, so often forgotten, empowers us to follow the vision of God into the future. Where God "has scattered the proud in the imagination of their hearts, he has put down the mighty from their thrones, and exalted those of low degree; he has filled the hungry with good things, and the rich he has sent empty away [Luke 1:51-53]."

---

*Saul D. Alinsky, *Rules for Radicals* (New York: Random House, 1971), p. 160.

†Quoted in *Signs of Shalom,* Edward A. Powers (Philadelphia: United Church Press), pp. 117–18, from *Engage,* 1972, pp. 13–20.

‡*The Coevolution Quarterly,* Fall 1975, edited by Stewart Brand (Box 428, Sausalito, CA 94065), p. 63.

PART THREE

SUPPORTIVE RESOURCES

A BIBLICAL LITANY: VISIONS AND STRATEGIES*

Visions

First Reader: "There will be no poor among you [for the voice of the Lord your God commands:] At the end of every seven years you shall grant a release . . . every creditor shall release what he has lent to his neighbor [Deut. 15:4, 1-2]."

"I do not mean that others should be eased and you burdened, but that as a matter of equality your abundance at the present time should supply their want, so that their abundance may supply your want, that there may be equality [2 Cor. 8:13-14]."

Second Reader: We envision redistribution of wealth and the world's goods so that the basic needs of all will be met.

All: Inform our vision, O Lord.

First Reader: "He shall judge between the nations and shall decide for many peoples; and they shall beat their swords into plowshares, and their spears into pruning hooks; nation shall not lift up sword against nation, neither shall they learn war any more [Isa. 2:4]."

Second Reader: We envision a world without war.

---

*Clara and William Rader, 1974. Printed in *JED Share—UCC*, February 1975. Copyrighted 1975 by United Church Press. Used by permission.

All: Inform our vision, O Lord.

First Reader: "The Spirit of the Lord . . . has anointed me to bring good tidings to the afflicted; . . . to proclaim liberty to the captives, and the opening of the prison to those who are bound [Isa. 61:1]."

Second Reader: We envision freedom for prisoners and victims of all kinds of oppression.

All: Inform our vision, O Lord.

First Reader: "Then he showed me the river of the water of life . . . [and] on either side of the river, the tree of life with its twelve kinds of fruit . . . and the leaves of the tree were for the healing of the nations [Rev. 22:1-2]."

Second Reader: We envision healing for physical sickness and for the sickness within and between nations.

All: Inform our vision, O Lord.

First Reader: "Behold, I create new heavens and a new earth; . . . no more shall be heard in it the sound of weeping and the cry of distress. . . . They shall build houses and inhabit them; they shall plant vineyards and eat their fruit. . . . They shall not hurt or destroy in all my holy mountain, says the Lord [Isa. 65:17, 19, 21, 25]."

Second Reader: We envision a new order of justice and peace, fellowship and creativity.

All: Inform our vision, O Lord.

Strategies

First Reader: "Love your enemies and pray for those who persecute you, so that you may be [children] of your Father who is in heaven [Matt. 5:44-45]."

Second Reader: Because our vision is one of love, our strategies must show love for those who oppose us.

All: Guide and strengthen us, O Lord.

First Reader: "You shall not hate your brother [or sister] in your heart, but you shall reason with your neighbor [Lev. 19:17]."

Second Reader: Our strategy is to treat those opposing us as persons, not things: to reason with them wherever possible; to appeal to their conscience and sense of responsibility.

All: Guide and strengthen us, O Lord.

First Reader: "Bless those who persecute you; bless and do not curse them . . . if your enemy is hungry, feed him; if he is thirsty, give him drink; for by so doing you will heap burning coals upon his head. Do not be overcome by evil, but overcome evil with good [Rom. 12:14, 20-21]."

All: Guide and strengthen us, O Lord.

First Reader: "Behold, I send you out as sheep in the midst of wolves; so be wise as serpents and innocent as doves [Matt. 10:16]."

Second Reader: Our strategy is to be as clever as possible in gathering all the relevant data and analyzing it thoroughly to understand both the problems which face us and the resources available.

All: Guide and strengthen us, O Lord.

First Reader: "Putting away falsehood, let every one speak the truth with his neighbor, for we are members one of another [Eph. 4:25]."

Second Reader: Our strategy is to initiate a flow of information that people may understand our goals and the forces that operate against them, victimizing all of us.

All: Guide and strengthen us, O Lord.

First Reader: "[Elijah said:] 'The people of Israel have forsaken thy covenant . . . and I, even I only, am left; and they seek my life, to take it away.' And the Lord said to him . . . 'I will leave seven thousand in Israel, all the knees that have not bowed to Baal' [1 Kings 19:14-15, 18]."

Second Reader: Our strategy is to locate all possible supporters, so that we need not complain of loneliness and isolation, but incorporate likely allies in a positive manner.

All: Guide and strengthen us, O Lord.

First Reader: "For just as the body is one and has many members, and all the members of the body, though many, are one body, so it is with Christ. . . . God has so adjusted the body . . . that there may be no discord in the body, but that the members may have the same care for one another. If one member suffers, all suffer together [1 Cor. 12:12, 24-26]."

Second Reader: Our strategy is to recognize that people have different possibilities of action, and that each is essential to the whole.

All: Guide and strengthen us, O Lord.

First Reader: " 'Lord, when did we see thee hungry and feed thee, or thirsty and give thee drink? And when did we see thee a stranger and welcome thee, or naked and clothe thee? And when did we see thee sick or in prison and visit thee?' And the King will answer them, 'Truly, I say to you, as you did it to one of the least of these my brethren, you did it to me [Matt. 25:37-40].' "

Second Reader: Our strategy is to stand with those in prison and in poverty, as Jesus shared our common lot.

All: Guide and strengthen us, O Lord.

First Reader: "We are not contending against flesh and blood, but against the principalities, against the powers, against the world rulers of this present darkness. . . . Christ Jesus . . . is our peace [Eph. 6:12; 2:13-14]."

THREE APPROACHES TO RELIGIOUS ISSUES

PERSONAL:
Religious groups have developed many skills, structures, and procedures for discovering the problems involved in personal lives. Besides theology, nearly all pastors take courses in pastoral psychology, which helps them "name the beasts" that oppress a person, such as alcoholism, loss of faith, depression, grief, or loneliness. The care of souls, counseling, ritual, all help minister to these needs.

INTERPERSONAL *(WITHIN SMALL GROUPS):*
We are also becoming more skilled in interpersonal work. Adding to centuries of experience with family relations and internal church relationships, the behavioral sciences have helped the church become more sensitive as to how people behave within small groups. With the ability to "name the beasts," the malfunctions that tyrannize a committee or organization (such as one-person rule, apathy, lack of ownership, endless monologues), we can begin to solve group-process problems with the skills of group dynamics.

INTERGROUP *(AMONG LARGE GROUPS):*
There is one area of desperate need that has only begun to surface as a church concern; that of the relations among groups, such as different races, nations, or economic groups. For the most part we have involved ourselves with either individual or interpersonal concerns. We have assumed that most moral difficulties were solvable on a personal or interpersonal level and have not fully recognized that problems often have an intergroup or large-group cause and solution.

We need to begin by analyzing how groups of people relate to each other. For example, one group of people often makes decisions for another group, and that situation is understood to be normal, appropriate, and natural, even God-given. Once we account for this, we begin to "tame the beasts" of large-group relationships the way we tame our personal ones.

THE GAS METER

This meter is an unscientific measuring tool by which to gauge what kind of response you are getting from the people in charge. It will measure thirteen different kinds of gas. The thirteen types are listed below with illustrations to help you develop your own sense of smell. They are verbal responses as opposed to actions, which we call social-control mechanisms.

1. *Shell Game:* If a choice is given to the dependent group the range is controlled. Example: "You can have higher prices or shortages. Take your pick."

2. *No Quotas:* Equal justice is supported over distributive justice, such as, in opposition to quotas or reparations. Example: "We would hire them, but they aren't qualified."

3. *Discredit Leadership:* A dependent group's leaders are discredited by insisting that they don't represent their people. Example: "Martin Luther had bowel trouble." Pharaoh tells the people, "Ignore his (Moses') lying words."

4. *Psychologism:* Name calling and personal attacks are used to avoid social problems. Example: "Gandhi was a masochist."

5. *Private Solutions:* Only private solutions are offered to public problems. Example: "Wear a sweater for the energy crisis"; "Let them eat cake"; "Let there be peace on earth and let it begin with *me*."

6. *Gobbledygook:* Technical or secret language or academic jargon is used to confuse people, such as on insurance policies, medical prescriptions, tax forms. Also called a "blast of fog" and "confusing the public." Example: "Subtract line 19c from 18a if deductions in 15e do not exceed item 4 in Schedule C."

7. *Pass the Buck:* Responsibility is denied and others blamed. Example: "The President was unaware of the burglary."

8. *Isolated Occurrence:* Patterns and policies of oppression are explained as unique accidents contrary to accepted policy. Example: "My Lai was an accident."

9. *Lie Like Crazy:* As a last resort, the skillful operator will simply state inaccurate or distorted information and do so with great authority. Example: "Fifty percent on welfare are chiselers."

10. *You Think This Is Bad:* Speaker attempts to lower expectations and make people thankful for small favors or nothing. Example: "Changing diapers at 50 cents an hour may not be a glamorous job, but just think of other people who are out of work." The action version of this verbal gas is "tighten the screw."

11. *Talk It to Death:* Filibusterer takes the floor to speak and simply uses up the available time by stalling, as a winning ball team controls the ball until time runs out.

12. *Change Terms:* Confronted with an abuse, the person switches the subject to a more comfortable topic. Example: "Senator, we don't want a nuclear plant in downtown Cedar Rapids." "Yes, Cedar Rapids is a beautiful city in springtime."

13. *Trickle Down:* People are promised that if they give up their power, wealth, or rights to those who already have it, more will trickle down to everybody. Example: "There will be more food for everyone if we turn agriculture over to a few big, efficient companies."

Now, take a speech, press conference, or response to a question which those in charge have made and:

1. Detect the type of gas it is.

2. Rate its pungency on a scale from 1 (meaning "smells fishy to me") to 10 (meaning "it burns my eyes").

3. Then rate each phrase.

BIBLICAL VISIONS OF THE GOOD WORLD: A SELECTED LIST

Leviticus	26:3-6
Isaiah	9:4-7
Psalm	72:2-7
Isaiah	11:2-9
Isaiah	42:2-9
Ezekiel	36:24-32
Matthew	5:3-12
Matthew	25:31-46
Luke	1:50-55
Revelation	21:1-4

CONTEMPORARY VISIONS

The Future: A Scenario*

There is a world out in space that is an exact duplication of our own. It is populated with men and women like ourselves. They live in countries like our own. They live under various economies and governments and are divided into different national, religious, and racial groups. They differ from us only in one respect. In each country there is a pathological obsession with human welfare.

As a result, over 60% of the national budgets are devoted to a compulsive and hysterical desire for sheltering life from the normal ravages of human existence which we accept more stoically. Billions of dollars are spent by governments on the conquest of disease. Over the years, nations have poured their resources into medical research and today no cancer, no kidney ailments, no degenerative disease exists.

Unheard of sums are spent by government on housing. They have so ordered their fiscal policies that slums and blight are unknown. They are so overprotective of their children that they overpay teachers, and the training schools for teachers have to turn away candidates. The perverseness of these conditions reaches its greatest height in their legislation against all private charities in behalf of human welfare. The outlawing of private charity has, of course, stifled the philanthropic instincts of the people.

There is only one exception to this restriction against private benevolence. Since the national budgets are so swollen with human betterment appropriations, there is little left for national defense. It therefore becomes necessary for private citizens to raise money for armaments. Thousands of private organizations exist for this purpose alone. There are clubs to buy guns through raffles. People stand with tin cups on street corners to collect coins for the purchase of hand grenades. Drives are conducted to acquire tanks. There are tag days for military aircraft. Cousin clubs sponsor dances to buy uniforms. The national governments simply neglect the problem of defense and let the burden fall on private agencies.

*The Future: "A Scenario" is reprinted from the handbook *You and the Nation's Priorities* by Ward L. Kaiser and Charles P. Lutz. N.Y.: Friendship Press, 1971. Used by permission.

But the inadequacy of this system is apparent to all. People grumble that under such a policy there will never be war.

I Have a Dream*

I say to you today, even though we face the difficulties of today and tomorrow, I still have a dream. It is a dream deeply rooted in the American Dream. I have a dream that one day this nation will rise up, live out the true meaning of its creed: "We hold these truths to be self-evident, that all men are created equal."

I have a dream that one day on the red hills of Georgia sons of former slaves and the sons of former slave-owners will be able to sit down together at the table of brotherhood. I have a dream that one day even the state of Mississippi, a state sweltering with the heat of injustice, sweltering with the heat of oppression, will be transformed into an oasis of freedom and justice.

I have a dream that my four little children will one day live in a nation where they will not be judged by the color of their skin but by the content of their character.

I have a dream that one day every valley shall be exalted, every hill and mountain shall be made low. The rough places will be made plain, and the crooked places will be made straight. This is the faith that I go back to the South with. With this faith we will be able to hew out of the mountain of despair a stone of hope. With this faith we will be able to work together, to pray together, to struggle together, to stand up for freedom together, knowing we will be free one day.

This will be the day when all of God's children will be able to sing with new meaning, "let freedom ring." So let freedom ring from the prodigious hilltops of New Hampshire. Let freedom ring from the mighty mountains of New York. But not only that. Let freedom ring from Stone Mountain of Georgia. Let freedom ring from every hill and molehill of Mississippi, from every mountain side.

When we allow freedom to ring—when we let it ring from every city and every hamlet, from every state and every city, we will be able to speed up that day when all of God's children, black men and white men, Jews and Gentiles, Protestants and Catholics, will be able to join hands and sing in the words of the old Negro spiritual, "Free at last, Free at last, Thank God almighty, we are free at last."

A Cooperative Model*

Women seek a reconstruction of relationships for which we have neither words nor models; a reconstruction which can give each person the fullness of their being stolen from them by false polarizations (male/female, soul/body, consciousness/nature, material/spiritual, sacred/secular, this world/the next, etc.) . . . and we must seek the fundamental reconstruction of the way resources are allocated within the world community. This implies a reconstruction of our basic models of interrelationships between persons, social groups, and finally, between humans and nature. Our model of relationships must cease to be hierarchical and become mutually supportive—a cooperative model of the fellowship of life systems.

---

*Excerpts from address by Martin Luther King, Jr. to the freedom marchers in Washington, D.C., in August 1963. Reprinted by permission of Joan Daves. Copyright © 1963 by Martin Luther King, Jr. Quoted from I Have a Dream. Time-Life Books, New York.

---

*Rosemary R. Ruether, New Woman, New Earth (New York: Seabury Press; Crossroads Books, 1975).

DECLARATION OF INDEPENDENCE

In Congress, July 4, 1776

The unanimous Declaration of the thirteen United States of America

When in the course of human events, it becomes necessary for one people to dissolve the political bands which have connected them with another, and to assume among the powers of the earth, the separate and equal station to which the Laws of Nature and of Nature's God entitle them, a decent respect to the opinions of mankind requires that they should declare the causes which impel them to the separation.

We hold these truths to be self-evident, that all men are created equal, that they are endowed by their Creator with certain inalienable rights, that among these are life, liberty, and the pursuit of happiness. That to secure these rights, governments are instituted among men, deriving their just powers from the consent of the governed, that whenever any form of government becomes destructive of these ends, it is the right of the people to alter or to abolish it, and to institute new government, laying its foundation on such principles, and organizing its powers in such form, as to them shall seem most likely to effect their safety and happiness. Prudence, indeed, will dictate that governments long established should not be changed for light and transient causes; and accordingly all experience hath shown, that mankind are more disposed to suffer, while evils are sufferable, than to right themselves by abolishing the forms to which they are accustomed. But when a long train of abuses and usurpations, pursuing invariably the same object, evinces a design to reduce them under absolute despotism, it is their right, it is their duty, to throw off such government, and to provide new guards for their future security. Such has been the patient sufferance of these Colonies; and such is now the necessity which constrains them to alter their former systems of government. The history of the present King of Great Britain is a history of repeated injuries and usurpations, all having in direct object the establishment of an absolute tyranny over these States. To prove this, let facts be submitted to a candid world.

He has refused his assent to laws, the most wholesome and necessary for the public good.

He has forbidden his Governors to pass laws of immediate and pressing importance, unless suspended in their operation till his assent should be obtained; and when so suspended, he has utterly neglected to attend to them.

He has refused to pass other laws for the accommodation of large districts of people, unless those people would relinquish the right of representation in the Legislature, a right inestimable to them, and formidable to tyrants only.

He has called together legislative bodies at places unusual, uncomfortable, and distant from the depository of their public records, for the sole purpose of fatiguing them into compliance with his measures.

He has dissolved representative houses repeatedly, for opposing with manly firmness his invasions on the rights of the people.

He has refused for a long time, after such dissolutions, to cause others to be elected; whereby the legislative powers, incapable of annihilation, have returned to the people at large for their exercise; the State remaining in the meantime exposed to all the dangers of invasion from without and convulsions within.

He has endeavoured to prevent the population of these States; for that purpose obstructing the laws for naturalization of foreigners; refusing to pass others to encourage their migrations hither, and raising the conditions of new appropriations of lands.

He has obstructed the administration of justice, by refusing his assent to laws for establishing judiciary powers.

He has made judges dependent on his will alone, for the tenure of their offices, and the amount and payment of their salaries.

He has erected a multitude of new offices, and sent hither swarms of officers to harass our people, and eat out their substance.

He has kept among us, in times of peace, standing armies without the consent of our legislatures.

He has affected to render the military independent of and superior to the civil power.

He has combined with others to subject us to a jurisdiction foreign to our constitution, and unacknowledged by our laws; giving his assent to their acts of pretended legislation:

For quartering large bodies of armed troops among us:

For protecting them, by a mock trial, from punishment for any murders which they should commit on the inhabitants of these States:

For cutting off our trade with all parts of the world:

For imposing taxes on us without our consent:

For depriving us, in many cases, of the benefits of trial by jury:

For transporting us beyond seas to be tried for pretended offences:

For abolishing the free system of English laws in a neighbouring Province, establishing therein an arbitrary government, and enlarging its boundaries, so as to render it at once an example and fit instrument for introducing the same absolute rule into these Colonies:

For taking away our Charters, abolishing our most valuable laws, and altering fundamentally the forms of our governments:

For suspending our own Legislatures, and declaring themselves invested with power to legislate for us in all cases whatsoever.

He has abdicated government here, by declaring us out of his protection and waging war against us.

He has plundered our seas, ravaged our coasts, burnt our towns, and destroyed the lives of our people.

He is, at this time, transporting large armies of foreign mercenaries to complete the works of death, desolation, and tyranny, already begun with circumstances of cruelty and perfidy scarcely paralleled in the most barbarous ages, and totally unworthy the head of a civilized nation.

He has constrained our fellow citizens taken captive on the high seas to bear arms against this country, to become the executioners of their friends and brethren, or to fall themselves by their hands.

He has excited domestic insurrections amongst us, and has endeavoured to bring on the inhabitants of our frontiers, the merciless Indian savages, whose known rule of warfare, is an undistinguished destruction, of all ages, sexes, and conditions.

In every stage of these oppressions we have petitioned for redress in the most humble terms: our repeated petitions have been answered only by repeated injury. A prince, whose character is thus marked by every act which may define a tyrant, is unfit to be the ruler of a free people.

Nor have we been wanting in attentions to our British brethren. We have warned them from time to time of attempts by their legislature to extend an unwarrantable jurisdiction over us. We have reminded them of the circumstances of our emigration and settlement here. We have appealed to their native justice and magnanimity, and we have conjured them by the ties of our common kindred to disavow these usurpations, which would inevitably interrupt our connections and correspondence. They too have been deaf to the voice of justice and of consanguinity. We must, therefore, acquiesce in the necessity, which denounces our separation, and hold them, as we hold the rest of mankind, enemies in war, in peace, friends.

We, therefore, the Representatives of the United States of America, in General Congress assembled, appealing to the Supreme Judge of the world for the rectitude of our intentions, do, in the name, and by authority of the good people of these Colonies, solemnly publish and declare, That these United Colonies are, and of right ought to be, Free and Independent States; that they are absolved from all allegiance to the British Crown, and that all political connection between them and the State of Great Britain, is and ought to be totally dissolved; and that as Free and Independent States, they have full power to levy war, conclude peace, contract alliances, establish commerce, and to do all other acts and things which Independent States may of right do. And for the support of this declaration, with a firm reliance on the protection of Divine Providence, we mutually pledge to each other our lives, our fortunes, and our sacred honor.

"ON ECONOMIC FREEDOM" BY JEREMY RIFKIN*

We hold these truths to be self-evident, that all people are created equal, that they are endowed by their Creator with certain inaliena- ble rights, that among these are life, liberty and the pursuit of happiness. That to secure these rights economic institutions are instituted among people, deriving their just power from the consent of the citizens; that whenever any economic system becomes destructive of these ends, it is the right of the people to alter or abolish it, and to institute a new economic system, laying its foundation on such prin- ciples, and organizing its powers in such form, as to them shall seem most likely to effect their safety and happiness. . . .

The history of the present economic system is a history of repeated injuries and usurpations, all having in direct object the establishment of an absolute tyranny over these states. To prove this, let the facts be submitted to a candid world:

America's giant corporations have seized control over the great land and resources of our country.

They have systematically destroyed thou- sands of small businesses and forced millions of Americans to become wage serfs for the wealthy owners.

They have turned one fifth of our nation into a weapons factory, wasting valuable labor and resources that could be utilized for basic human needs.

They have formed shared monopolies in vir- tually every major retail and wholesale industry, forcing millions of consumers to pay higher and higher prices for goods and services they can- not do without—these monopoly practices being the primary cause of runaway inflation.

They have forced millions of workers into unemployment lines by systematically closing down their American plants and moving their business operations abroad so they can hire cheap foreign labor.

The giant corporations have subverted the Constitution and the principle of Government of, by and for the people by the following means:

Illegally financing their own candidates for local, state and national office.

Placing their own supporters in key Govern- ment commissions and regulatory agencies.

Using massive lobbying operations to vir- tually dictate the legislative direction of the state and Federal Governments, including the deci- sions on how our tax money is allocated.

These same corporate giants also:

Profess the strongest attachment to self- reliance while pocketing billions of dollars of our tax money in the form of Government subsidies and special favors.

Herald the virtues of personal responsibility and accountability, while engaging in wholesale crime under the protection of their corporate charters.

America's giant corporations have issued a death sentence against the individual human spirit by forcing millions of Americans to perform mind- less functions eight hours a day inside the corpo- rate machine, and by rewarding obedience, con- formity, and dependency—and penalizing creative thinking, criticism, and independent judgment.

The corporate giants have violated our sacred rights to life, liberty and the pursuit of happiness by denying us adequate access to the means to sus- tain life, and by denying us a range of work choices that are potentially self-fulfilling and rewarding.

In their obsession with profits, their lust for absolute dominion over the life of this nation, and their total disregard for the people, corporate owners and managers have plunged our country into its present state of economic chaos, destroyed the lives of millions of families, and threatened the very survival of the Republic.

In every stage of these oppressions, we have petitioned for redress in the most humble terms; our repeated petitions have been answered only by repeated injury. An economic system whose character is marked by every act that may define an absolute tyranny is unfit to claim the loyalty and allegiance of a free and democratic people.

We, therefore, the citizens of the United States of America, hereby call for the abolition of these giant institutions of tyranny and the establishment of new economic enterprises to provide for the equal and democratic participation of all American citizens in the economic decisions that affect the well-being of our families, our communities and our nation.

In furtherance of our joint hopes and aspira-

*Copyright © 1975 by The New York Times Company. Reprinted by permission. Jeremy Rifkin, economist and co-di- rector of the People's Bicentennial Commission, is author of "Common Sense II." (*The New York Times,* Monday, May 26, 1975.)

tions, and mindful of the lessons of history, we steadfastly adhere to the general principle that a democratic republic can only exist to the extent that economic decision-making power is broadly exercised by the people and not delegated to a few.

Such is the necessity which compels us to act in support of decentralized economic enterprises, with ownership and control being shared jointly by the workers in the plants and by the local communities in which they operate—with similar patterns of shared representative control being exercised on a regional and national level to insure the smooth and efficient coordination of all economic operations.

For the support of this declaration, with a firm reliance on the protection of Divine Providence, we mutually pledge our lives, our fortunes, and our most sacred honor.

QUESTIONNAIRE ON APPLIED RIGHTS

(Please answer yes, no, or don't know to the following questions.)

	Yes	No	Don't Know
Article I			
1. Do you believe that the government should avoid any special help, assistance, or favored treatment to any religious group even if it's a majority?			
2. Should all religious sects be allowed to practice their type of beliefs, whatever they are, as long as they hurt no one?			
3. Should people be allowed to say anything they please in public and in the press?			
4. Should people be allowed to gather into huge throngs to ask the government to change laws?			
Article II			
1. Should individuals be allowed to keep guns solely for the purpose of possible organized military action if called upon?			
Article III			
1. Should a homeowner be allowed to remove a soldier or FBI agent from his/her house if he or she wants to?			
Article IV			
1. In order to search one's house, letters, and personal effects, should the police or FBI be required to show probable cause of suspicion which is backed up by sworn statements and all kinds of details about persons, places, and things to be searched?			
Article V			
1. Should the police be forced to get indictments from a grand jury for a major crime before they can hold anyone for questioning?			
2. If a person is judged innocent in a trial but is later shown to be guilty, should that person be tried again?			
3. Should a person on trial for a crime be compelled to tell the whole truth even against himself or herself?			
4. Should the police detain a person or take his or her property if he or she looks suspicious, even though the police officer has not gone through channels?			
5. If the government needs land for a highway or other government project and the owner resists, should the government take it away from the owner without any more bother?			
Article VI			
1. Should a person suspected of a crime be able to demand a lawyer and witnesses to help him or her, be told of all the things he or she is accused of, and have a speedy public trial?			
Article VII			
1. Should all trials involving criminal or civil cases of a dispute of, say, $20 or more be tried with a jury if the people want it?			
Article VIII			
1. Should there be a limit to the bail, fines, and treatment of a mass murderer?			
Article IX			
1. Should the people and the States have any and all rights and powers that the U.S. Constitution does not claim?			

VISIONARIES' CHECKLIST

(Even visionaries forget an item or two when they are off dreaming and visioning. Next time you go to the wilderness to get pure and to have fantasies, don't forget this friendly reminder.)
Have you forgotten to dream about:

Oh Yes!	Already Included	Not Interested	
☐	☐	☐	1. Jobs, employment, under what conditions
☐	☐	☐	2. Consumer protection and prices for goods
☐	☐	☐	3. Taxes
☐	☐	☐	4. Discrimination
☐	☐	☐	5. Hunger, malnutrition
☐	☐	☐	6. Housing
☐	☐	☐	7. Education
☐	☐	☐	8. Health care
☐	☐	☐	9. Corporate responsibility
☐	☐	☐	10. Environmental protection
☐	☐	☐	11. Urban needs
☐	☐	☐	12. Transportation
☐	☐	☐	13. Military spending
☐	☐	☐	14. Retirement and pensions
☐	☐	☐	15. Energy consumption
☐	☐	☐	16. Equality between women and men
☐	☐	☐	17. Land use
☐	☐	☐	18. Equal opportunity

THE ECONOMIC BILL OF RIGHTS

We, the People of the United States, advancing into the third century of our nation's existence, do hereby proclaim this Economic Bill of Rights and pledge ourselves to judge future Presidents and Members of Congress, as well as state and local governments, on how effectively they adhere to its principles and implement its purposes.

Article I: Every person who is able and willing to work shall have the right to a job at a livable wage under decent working conditions.

Article II: Consumers shall be protected against excessive prices, unwarranted interest charges, fraudulent and misleading advertisements, adulterated and hazardous products, shoddy workmanship, and other abuses.

Article III: Tax laws shall be revised to conform to the ability-to-pay principle: tax loopholes for wealthy persons and corporations shall be closed; the neediest shall be given priority in tax relief.

Article IV: There shall be no discrimination against any person in regard to employment, pay standards, training, promotion and other economic opportunities because of race, sex, religion or other extraneous factors. Where inequities exist, they shall be rectified.

Article V: The government shall take the necessary steps to eliminate hunger, malnutrition, and poverty in our country and help to alleviate starvation among the world's poor. It shall see that food, energy, and other essentials are made available in sufficient quantities and at reasonable prices.

Article VI: Every person shall have the right to adequate housing, education, medical care, and other requirements for a humane existence. The government shall ensure that funds, facilities, and staffing for these services are expanded in accordance with the growing needs of the population.

Article VII: Industrial and financial corporations shall be held accountable for the manner in which their operations and policies serve the people. When they act contrary to the public interest, they shall be placed under public ownership, with due compensation to their stockholders.

Article VIII: The government shall give high priority to social, educational, and environmental programs that enrich the lives of the people, make our cities more habitable, and create new job opportunities. Military spending shall be reduced to levels consistent with national defense.

Article IX: People shall have the right to a decent livelihood while they are working and to an adequate pension when they retire. Needy persons who are incapable of working shall have the right to a subsistence income.

Article X: International trade shall be conducted with due regard to the needs of consumers, workers, farmers, and small businesses. Multinational corporations shall not be permitted to undermine the wage standards and job opportunities of working people.

AMENDMENTS TO THE CONSTITUTION

ARTICLES I-X (THE BILL OF RIGHTS), 1791

Article I
Congress shall make no law respecting an establishment of religion, or prohibiting the free exercise thereof; or abridging the freedom of speech, or of the press; or the right of the people peaceably to assemble, and to petition the Government for a redress of grievances.

Article II
A well-regulated militia being necessary to the security of a free State, the right of the people to keep and bear arms shall not be infringed.

Article III
No soldier shall, in time of peace be quartered in any house, without the consent of the owner, nor in time of war, but in a manner to be prescribed by law.

Article IV
The right of the people to be secure in their persons, houses, papers, and effects, against unreasonable searches and seizures, shall not be violated, and no warrants shall issue, but upon probable cause, supported by oath or affirmation, and particularly describing the place to be searched, and the persons or things to be seized.

Article V
No person shall be held to answer for a capital, or otherwise infamous crime, unless on a presentment or indictment of a grand jury, except in cases arising in the land or naval forces, or in the militia, when in actual service in time of war or public danger; nor shall any person be subject for the same offence to be twice put in jeopardy of life or limb; nor shall be compelled in any criminal case to be a witness against himself, nor be deprived of life, liberty, or property, without due process of law; nor shall private property be taken for public use, without just compensation.

Article VI
In all criminal prosecutions, the accused shall enjoy the right to a speedy and public trial, by an impartial jury of the State and district wherein the crime shall have been committed, which district shall have been previously ascertained by law, and to be informed of the nature and cause of the accusation; to be confronted with the witness against him; to have compulsory process for obtaining witnesses in his favor, and to have the assistance of counsel for his defense.

Article VII
In suits at common law, where the value in controversy shall exceed twenty dollars, the right of trial by jury shall be preserved, and no fact tried by a jury shall be otherwise re-examined in any court of the United States, than according to the rules of the common law.

Article VIII
Excessive bail shall not be required, nor excessive fines imposed, nor cruel and unusual punishments inflicted.

Article IX
The enumeration in the Constitution, of certain rights, shall not be construed to deny or disparage others retained by the people.

Article X
The powers not delegated to the United States by the Constitution, nor prohibited by it to the States, are reserved to the States respectively, or to the people.

WRITING AN EFFECTIVE LETTER*

"If the average member of Congress received as many as a half-dozen letters scrawled in pencil on brown wrapping paper, it would be enough to change his or her vote on most issues," a government official, veteran of about twenty years on Capitol Hill, once said. He may have exaggerated, but his statement indicates that members of Congress want to know how ordinary people in their districts feel about public questions. Responsible citizens should write often; their letters should be in good form and contain compelling reasoning. Here are a few suggestions for writing an effective letter to a national official:

1. Keep each letter reasonably brief and limit the subject matter to a single issue. When writing about legislation, refer to the accurate title and number of the bill.

2. Point up the moral issues involved. Specify why you are personally advocating a particular position. If an organization to which you belong has taken an official action on the issue, you may want to refer to that. Let the government official know that you are concerned and informed. Make your communication your own and not a form letter.

3. Be positive. Avoid criticism. If possible, compliment the legislator on some recent action, vote, or public speech. Occasionally devote your entire letter to praise for some constructive proposal or action.

4. To get a personal response, ask a thoughtful question about an issue which concerns you. Ask for the legislator's opinion or, after you have stated your opinion, write, "Can I count on your support on this vital matter?"

5. Point out shortcomings which you have noted in a particular bill and make suggestions for correcting these.

CORRECT FORMS OF ADDRESS FOR U.S. GOVERNMENT OFFICIALS*

The President: The President
    The White House
    Washington, D.C. 20500
Mr. President:

Senators: The Honorable ——— ———
    United States Senate
    Washington, D.C. 20510
Dear Senator ———:

Members of the House of Representatives: The Honorable ——— ——— ———
    House of Representatives
    Washington, D.C. 20510
Dear Mr. (Miss, Mrs., Ms.) ———:

Members of the Cabinet: The Honorable ———
——— ———
    (Correct title, such as "Secretary of State")
    (Correct department, such as "State Department")
    Washington, D.C. 20510
Dear Mr. (Ms.) Secretary ———:

Members of the Judiciary:
    The Honorable ——— ———
    (Title: Chief Justice or Associate Justice)
    United States Supreme Court
    Washington, D.C. 20543
Dear Mr. (Ms.) Justice:
    or
Dear Mr. (Ms.) Chief Justice: (when addressing this officer)

U.S. Mission to the United Nations:
    The Honorable ——— ———
    U.S. Mission to the U.N.
    799 United Nations Plaza
    New York, N.Y. 10017

*From Congressional Staff Directory.

*From Congressional Staff Directory.

FORMS OF ADDRESS FOR CANADIAN GOVERNMENT OFFICIALS*

GOVERNMENT

The Governor General (if the name is used):
   His Excellency —— ——
   Government House
   Ottawa
If a member of the Queen's Privy Council for Canada:
   His Excellency the Honourable —— ——
If a member of Her Majesty's Most Honourable Privy Council (The United Kingdom Privy Council):
   His Excellency the Right Honourable—— ——.

Salutation and Closing:
Sir: *or* Madam:
I have the honour to be, Sir *or* Madam,
Your Excellency's obedient servant.
or Dear Governor General:
Believe me, Your Excellency.
Yours sincerely.

LIEUTENANT-GOVERNOR OF A PROVINCE:

   His Honour, The Lieutenant-Governor of (the Province of) ——
   Government House ——
Salutation and Closing:
Sir: *or* Madam:
I am, Your Honour.
Yours very truly.

THE PRIME MINISTER OF CANADA:

   The Right Honourable —— ——, P.C., M.P.
   Minister of Canada
   Ottawa. KIA 0A6
Salutation and Closing:
Dear Sir: *or* Dear Madam:
Yours very truly.

THE PREMIER OF A PROVINCE OF CANADA:

   The Honourable —— —— M.L.A.
   Premier of the Province of ——
Salutation and Closing:
Dear Sir: *or* Dear Madam:
Yours very truly.

MEMBER OF THE SENATE:

   The Honourable —— ——
   The Senate, Ottawa.
Salutation and Closing:
Dear Sir: *or* Dear Madam:
Yours very truly.

MEMBERS OF THE HOUSE OF COMMONS:

   —— ——, Esq. M.P.
   House of Commons, Ottawa.
Salutation and Closing:
Dear Sir: *or* Dear Madam:
Yours very truly.

DEPUTY MINISTER OF A DEPARTMENT:

   —— ——, Esq. Deputy Minister of ——
Salutation and Closing:
Sir: *or* Madam:
Yours truly.

MEMBER OF A PROVINCIAL GOVERNMENT:

   —— ——, Esq. M.L.A.
   Member of the Legislative Assembly
   (Legislative Bldgs., Edmonton; Parliament Bldgs., Victoria; Legislative Bldg., Winnipeg; Legislative Bldg., Fredericton; Confederation Bldg., St. John's Province House, Halifax; Parliament Bldgs., Toronto; Province Bldg., Charlottetown; Hotel de Gouvernment, Quebec; Legislative Bldgs., Regina).
Salutation and Closing:
Dear Sir: *or* Dear Madam:
Yours very truly.

MAYOR OF A CITY OR TOWN:

   His Worship Mayor —— ——, *or* Her Worship Mayor —— ——
   City Hall.
Salutation and Closing:
Dear Sir: *or* Dear Madam:
Yours very truly.

---

*Used by permission of Macmillan Co. of Canada, from *Styles of Addresses* by Howard Measures. Suggested by Neil Topliffe.

A SIMPLE PLANNING TOOL

One of the simplest forms of planning an action is to ask yourself and your group six questions: What, Why, When, Where, How, Who? This is so simple that it is especially good for people who are not yet thinking in goals/objectives planning categories. It's also useful in midstream of an action process. Even these questions, however, must be focused on the things you want to accomplish.

Name a concern you have, one you know something about, so that the facts are well established:

_____

_____

_____

_____

What . . . are we doing or going to do about it?

_____

_____

_____

_____

_____

This question pinpoints what you are about. Or if you're not yet organized, it forces a decision and possible agreement in the group on what exactly you are going to try to accomplish. It answers your critics, who doubt whether you "know what you are doing." Remember the British military commander in the story *Bridge over the River Kwai* who built the bridge for the Japanese during World War II. He got so involved in *how* to do it, he forgot *what* it was all about and fought off his countrymen who tried to destroy the bridge. Do you know what you want and what you are doing to get it?

_____

_____

_____

_____

_____

Jesus saw people who were lost because they did not know what was up. They were hopping all around, getting anxious, trying to gain the whole world but losing their souls. What's it all about, Zaccheus?

Why . . . are we doing it or going to do it?

_____

_____

_____

_____

This question could get you into a Hamlet fit, so watch it. The question "why" suggests all kinds of deep theological issues, but in a social change context it merely means: *Why* are we doing this in the context of our action goals? *Why* are we boycotting fudgesicle when the issue is popsicle? Why campaign for your party's choice when you know he or she is dishonest? When planning an action, appoint an obnoxious child to keep asking "Why?" It keeps you honest.

When . . . are we going to do it?

_____

_____

_____

_____

_____

This *when* question is the supreme test of The Gas Meter. Those in charge, and the down-and-outs too, are full of promises they will keep in some distant future. When you ask when (which millennium? year? month? day? hour?), watch the meter fall and the squirming rise. If your group is all spirited up ready for action, it's time to set dates and, next . . . place.

Where . . . will it happen?

_____

_____

_____

_____

_____

The exact location has to be pinned down too. When you agree on where you will take action, that requires all kinds of special arrangements peculiar to that location. Where it happens affects the people's "turf" you are invading. You've got to know where you are going.

How . . . are we going to get to our *what?*

_____

_____

_____

_____

_____

This questions bursts a lot of hot air balloons. The *how* question is a reality tester. It makes mush of our fantasies. "How are you going to end hunger?" is a practical question that forces us to cut our plans down to size and do possible things. It also forces us to chart out step by step a "how to" plan of action.

Who . . . is going to do which part?

_____

_____

_____

_____

_____

Now, in any meeting that's full of big ideas, you will see people diving under the table when you ask "who" will take minutes or call the mayor's office or whatever. But everybody's job is nobody's job! Pin all the plans down to one accountable soul and table the rest, because without a *who* forget the *whats.*

SPOTTING POWER POLITICS

How do you know when you are being cheated or exploited? There are some clear verbal signals we are aware of when the con artist and the flimflam man try to sell us tickets to Mars or shares in desert real estate. However, on a social, large-group level, a new set of mechanisms is at work (or play), the knowledge of which helps prevent exploitation.

There are many verbal signals that give away the tactics of power politics. Here is a match up exercise to help you polish your skill at spotting the tactics of power politics.

On the left are some phrases that signal that the speaker may assume a dominant/dependent perspective and thus use this power tactic. See if you can match up these phrases with the tactics on the right side. You may want to read over the Background Readings on Using Power.

THE TACTICS OF POWER POLITICS

Verbal Signals   *Social-Control Mechanisms*

Rewards

1. "Let us make those hard investment decisions for you" and "Go along to get along."
2. "Woman's place is in the home" and "I give up, you can't fight City Hall."
3. "Ladies first" and "Fred, I bet you say that to all the girls."
4. "Be a good team man" and "First I'll get rich, then I'll help the poor."
5. "A few drugs will quiet them down" and "We have a soft life here, why spoil it?"
6. "Give a good show and let them eat cake" and "When my luck changes, I'll be a winner."
7. "It's for your own protection" and "I promise to love and obey."
8. "And now the Boston Pops brings you an evening of Negro spirituals" and "My name is Mrs. John Oliver Oldhain, Jr."
9. "Let us send a basket to the poor" and "Master's been so kind to me."

a. Slavery's Normal and That's Life
b. Decider's Rule and Follow the Leader
c. Protection and Obedience
d. Pedestal and Flattery
e. Steal Culture and Deny Identity
f. Cooptation and Privateer
g. Enforce Decadence and Fleshpot
h. Bread and Circuses and Magic, Miracle, and Chance
i. Band-Aid and Thank-youthankyou

Punishments

10. "You can't do it, ask an expert" and "Yes, I'm too stupid."
11. "Women are emotional" and "I'm only a housewife."
12. "We have decided to move you to your own area" and "I know where I belong."
13. "These people are asking for trouble" and "I'm as bad as the next one."
14. "Forget them, they don't count" and "If you are quiet, no one will notice."
15. "The poor have no one but themselves to blame" and "It's our own fault."
16. "If we speed up the production line, they will forget their problems" and "At least we still have our jobs."

j. Apartheid and Know My Place
k. Limit Access and Play Dumb
l. Stereotype and Introjection
m. Blame the Victim and Blame Self
n. Pit the Victim and Fight Each Other
o. Tighten the Screw and Gratitude for Small Favors
p. Zap and Vanish

There are many more example phrases you can think of. List additional ones. Compare your answers and list others to further polish your skill in spotting power politics.

The answers are:

1-b, 2-a, 3-d, 4-f, 5-g, 6-h, 7-c, 8-e, 9-i, 10-k, 11-l, 12-j, 13-n, 14-p, 15-m, 16-o.

THE CHANGE CHART
Areas of Desired Change

Types of Action	Social/Cultural	Economic	Political
Protest			
Persuasion			
Noncooperation			
Intervention			

This chart is adapted from Gene Sharp's *The Politics of Nonviolent Action;* Sharp's list of 194 possible actions is reprinted on pages 135–37. This should help people sort out what types of actions they want. To build group pride, a social/cultural protest might be chosen, such as a "we are somebody" march. Or if the group is unified, a mass economic noncooperation action like the Montgomery boycott may be selected. A sit-in at the White House would be called a "political intervention."

LIBERATOR'S TOOL KIT

The liberator's tool kit is made up of a number of things people can draw on to help them accomplish something. People who intend to follow Jesus' mission of liberating the oppressed (Luke 4:18) will have the following advantages and possibilities.

1. *Jesus.* First of all, Jesus is not a tool. But Jesus can be called on because he is the ideal liberator. Acting with pure moral power, he changed the world. He is a source of inspiration, guidance, and an example to people of militant, nonviolent action, words, and life. Jesus relieves people of the burden of looking around for new heroes, leaders, and saviors to follow who will take away their burdens. Liberation is not given away by compassionate leaders; it is developed by people taking charge of their own lives and aiding others to do the same, as Jesus did.

2. *Moral Power.* Moral power is the main tool in the Liberator's Tool Kit. It rests not on the "consent of the governed," as democratic political power does, but upon the human liberation of people to rule themselves. Moral power is a nonviolent win-win approach to change that uses means that are consistent with its end of a humane world. This is also distinct from power politics, which is a win/lose approach with power (as such) as its goal and no moral limits to the means of reaching that goal. It is also distinct from moralistic power, which only worries about personal purity.

3. *Numbers.* People who are dominated by others often outnumber them. The rulers are able to rule not only because they control the political and military forces, but also because the dominated group lets it happen. They cooperate by playing slave to the tyrant. When they get tired of this role, they can start counting all the numbers of people who may join in refusing to cooperate with the ruler. Large numbers of people are hard to control.

4. *Noncooperation.* Dominated people rarely see that the tyrant needs and depends on their cooperation in the tyranny. But once the cooperation stops, the house of cards begins to shake.

5. *Little to Lose.* Groups who control a society to the exclusion of other dominated people feel they have "everything to lose" from social change. Dominated people do not. The "little to lose" attitude is liberating when it's fully developed. It makes you not "anxious about your life [Matt. 6:25]." Courage to make changes comes from this attitude. By contrast, those who "lay up . . . treasures on earth" have to do constant battle with moths, rust, thieves, and liberated people (Matthew 6:19).

6. *Flexibility.* If you don't have many "treasures on earth" and little to lose to the moths, rust, and thieves, then you can be more flexible. You are not tied down to the maintenance of institutions the way the tyrants are. Your average tyrant's daily life is full of hassles, palace revolts, assassinations, etc. It's a drag.

7. *Incorruptibility.* In order to be more flexible, and less anxious, and to refuse to cooperate in one's own oppression, you must not want or need what the tyrant has got, i.e., treasures on earth. The tyrant's power corrupts him or her, but it also corrupts everybody else who craves the tyrant's values and treasures. Liberation requires a complete change in people's desires away from the "treasures" which corrupt to the treasures which liberate.

8. *Patience.* The oppressed have to endure suffering. This can be spiritually destructive if one has the tyrant's values. But "suffering produces endurance, and endurance produces character, and character produces hope [Rom. 5:4]." If one has Jesus' values, then suffering, like hard work, makes you strong.

9. *Unity.* The most powerful tool for change is the spiritual bond of love that unites a people in a good cause. The tyrant finds spiritual, nonphysical tools hard to fight and destroy. Unity is essential for liberation. That is why tyrants work so hard at pitting the victims against each other. Tyrants have no tools to defend themselves against love.

10. *The Future.* The "gentle shall inherit the earth." Liberation is a future promise to the dominated people. The rich and powerful already "have their reward." The dominated live on hope. They "consider the little children" and expect great things from the Lord in future generations.

HOW TO VISIT A LEGISLATOR

1. Call ahead for an appointment. Be persistent but polite.
2. Get your group organized. Appoint a spokesperson.
3. Prepare your arguments well.
4. Be firm but polite.
5. Do not threaten, beg, or get emotional.
6. Do not be gullible either.
7. Patiently make your case and keep the legislator on the subject.
8. Limit your issues to one or two.
9. The legislator usually wants to please you, but also the other people who keep him or her in office.
10. Leave your names, addresses, and written arguments.

METHODS OF NONVIOLENT ACTION

The following list of methods is the detailed table of contents of Part Two of Gene Sharp's *The Politics of Nonviolent Action,* single volume hardback, 1973, and three-volume paperback: *Power and Struggle, The Methods of Nonviolent Action,* and *The Dynamics of Nonviolent Action,* 1973. Porter Sargent Publishers, Inc., 11 Beacon Street, Boston, Massachusetts 02108.

THE METHODS OF NONVIOLENT PROTEST AND PERSUASION

FORMAL STATEMENTS
1. Public speeches
2. Letters of opposition or support
3. Declarations by organizations and institutions
4. Signed public statements
5. Declarations of indictment and intention
6. Group or mass petitions

COMMUNICATIONS WITH A WIDER AUDIENCE
7. Slogans, caricatures, and symbols
8. Banners, posters, and displayed communications
9. Leaflets, pamphlets, and books
10. Newspapers and journals
11. Records, radio, and television
12. Skywriting and earthwriting

GROUP REPRESENTATIONS
13. Deputations
14. Mock awards
15. Group lobbying
16. Picketing
17. Mock elections

SYMBOLIC PUBLIC ACTS
18. Displays of flags and symbolic colors
19. Wearing of symbols
20. Prayer and worship
21. Delivering symbolic objects
22. Protest disrobings
23. Destruction of own property
24. Symbolic lights
25. Displays of portraits
26. Paint as protest
27. New signs and names
28. Symbolic sounds
29. Symbolic reclamations
30. Rude gestures

PRESSURES ON INDIVIDUALS
31. "Haunting" officials
32. Taunting officials
33. Fraternization
34. Vigils

DRAMA AND MUSIC
35. Humorous skits and pranks
36. Performances of plays and music
37. Singing

PROCESSIONS
38. Marches
39. Parades
40. Religious processions
41. Pilgrimages
42. Motorcades

HONORING THE DEAD
43. Political mourning
44. Mock funerals
45. Demonstrative funerals
46. Homage at burial places

PUBLIC ASSEMBLIES
47. Assemblies of protest or support
48. Protest meetings
49. Camouflaged meetings of protest
50. Teach-ins

WITHDRAWAL AND RENUNCIATION
51. Walk-outs
52. Silence
53. Renouncing honors
54. Turning one's back

THE METHODS OF SOCIAL NONCOOPERATION

OSTRACISM OF PERSONS
55. Social boycott
56. Selective social boycott
57. Lysistratic nonaction
58. Excommunication
59. Interdict

NONCOOPERATION WITH SOCIAL EVENTS, CUSTOMS AND INSTITUTIONS
60. Suspension of social and sports activities
61. Boycott of social affairs
62. Student strike
63. Social disobedience
64. Withdrawal from social institutions

WITHDRAWAL FROM THE SOCIAL SYSTEM
65. Stay-at-home
66. Total personal noncooperation
67. "Flight" of workers
68. Sanctuary
69. Collective disappearance
70. Protest emigration *(hijrat)*

THE METHODS OF ECONOMIC NONCOOPERATION: (1) ECONOMIC BOYCOTTS

ACTION BY CONSUMERS
71. Consumers' boycott
72. Nonconsumption of boycotted goods
73. Policy of austerity
74. Rent withholding
75. Refusal to rent
76. National consumers' boycott
77. International consumers' boycott

ACTION BY WORKERS AND PRODUCERS
78. Workmen's boycott
79. Producers' boycott

ACTION BY MIDDLEMEN
80. Suppliers' and handlers' boycott

ACTION BY OWNERS AND MANAGEMENT
81. Traders' boycott
82. Refusal to let or sell property
83. Lockout
84. Refusal of industrial assistance
85. Merchants' "general strike"

ACTION BY HOLDERS OF FINANCIAL RE-SOURCES
86. Withdrawal of bank deposits
87. Refusal to pay fees, dues, and assessments
88. Refusal to pay debts or interest
89. Severance of funds and credit
90. Revenue refusal
91. Refusal of a government's money

ACTION BY GOVERNMENTS
92. Domestic embargo
93. Blacklisting of traders
94. International sellers' embargo
95. International buyers' embargo
96. International trade embargo

THE METHODS OF ECONOMIC NONCOOPERATION: (2) THE STRIKE

SYMBOLIC STRIKES
97. Protest strike
98. Quickie walkout (lightning strike)

AGRICULTURAL STRIKES
99. Peasant strike
100. Farm workers' strike

STRIKES BY SPECIAL GROUPS
101. Refusal of impressed labor
102. Prisoners' strike
103. Craft strike
104. Professional strike

ORDINARY INDUSTRIAL STRIKES
105. Establishment strike
106. Industry strike
107. Sympathetic strike

RESTRICTED STRIKES
108. Detailed strike
109. Bumper strike
110. Slowdown strike
111. Working-to-rule strike
112. Reporting "sick" (sick-in)
113. Strike by resignation
114. Limited strike
115. Selective strike

MULTI-INDUSTRY STRIKES
116. Generalized strike
117. General strike

COMBINATION OF STRIKES AND ECONOMIC CLOSURES
118. Hartal
119. Economic shutdown

THE METHODS OF POLITICAL NONCOOPERATION

REJECTION OF AUTHORITY
120. Withholding or withdrawal of allegiance
121. Refusal of public support
122. Literature and speeches advocating resistance

CITIZENS' NONCOOPERATION WITH GOVERNMENT
123. Boycott of legislative bodies
124. Boycott of elections
125. Boycott of government employment and positions
126. Boycott of government departments, agencies, and other bodies
127. Withdrawal from government educational institutions
128. Boycott of government-supported organizations
129. Refusal of assistance to enforcement agents
130. Removal of own signs and placemarks
131. Refusal to accept appointed officials
132. Refusal to dissolve existing institutions

CITIZENS' ALTERNATIVES TO OBEDIENCE
133. Reluctant and slow compliance
134. Nonobedience in absence of direct supervision
135. Popular nonobedience
136. Disguised disobedience
137. Refusal of an assemblage or meeting to disperse
138. Sitdown
139. Noncooperation with conscription and deportation

CARDINAL RULES FOR MAKING CHANGE

1. The first rule of social change is: Don't take power personally. Meaning: (a) Don't bother doing it alone. and (b) Don't get over emotional.

2. Don't play Hamlet. He's on a head trip. He could not decide to be or not to be, so he decided by default. Not to decide and act is to decide and act in favor of the status quo, i.e., to resist change.

3. Only action counts. The score is not kept on feelings and emotions or profound ideas but on action that makes a difference.

4. Discontent is no sin. If you are contented, go chew your cud. Social change happens because a number of people are discontented and get organized and act.

5. Decide exactly what you want to get done. One single item is best. Two will bring more people in but dilutes it. Three gets fuzzy. You won't be able to remember four. Keep it exact, clear, so you can remember it—if you go to jail.

6. Keep it simple so everybody, your people and your adversary, can't forget it.

7. Never make your adversary your personal enemy. He or she may join your group on the next issue. All people are respectable human beings. Pay respect to that humanity. "Love your adversary," says the Lord. But the Lord did not say love anything that person stands for or on. And don't give your adversary the excuse of making you a personal enemy.

8. Keep asking, "What are we doing?" Is this essential now, according to our plan, or is it a side track? Be able to answer what, why, when, where, how, who questions at all times.

9. Know your adversary well and his or her needs and wants, plans and goals. This is not to be manipulative. It is to help you know which item he or she will give up and which are nonnegotiable.

10. Keep your Gas Meter working. Learn to smell gas immediately—that is, gobbledygook, shell game, Band-Aid, etc. Be ready to counteract them.

11. Don't worry, plan. Worry is what people do about things they can't change. Of course, people *will* worry, and this must be handled with personal counseling and/or small-group work. This is important, but don't confuse it with action, change, or society.

SELECTED BIBLIOGRAPHY

This is a list of a few of the most helpful books that are referred to in the notebook. They are recommended for future reading.

THEOLOGY

Alves, Rubem A. *A Theology of Human Hope.* Washington: Corpus Book, 1969.

A complex book, but one of the first breakthroughs in the interpretation of theology from a social perspective. It helped launch liberation theology by reevaluating and moving beyond the dominant theologians of the last forty years.

Alves, Rubem A. *Tomorrow's Child: Imagination, Creativity, and the Rebirth of Culture.* New York: Harper and Row, 1972.

Alves gives very insightful analysis of social and cultural powers that thwart liberation. His hope does not lie in an exodus, rather he opts for the biblical image of exile in Babylon, in the heart of the enemy.

Brueggmann, Walter. *Living Toward a Vision.* Philadelphia: United Church Press, 1976.

A book of inspiring reflections which give a biblical perspective on social change. It illuminates both the need for and the content of visions for the future.

Gutierrez, Gustavo. *A Theology of Liberation.* Translated by Sister Caridad Inda and John Eagleson. Maryknoll, N.Y.: Orbis Books, 1971.

The central theological interpretation of Christianity from a South American revolutionary perspective. It systematically lays out basic Christian teaching from a perspective of Third World liberation.

Otto, Rudolf. *The Idea of the Holy.* Translated by John W. Harvey. New York: Oxford University Press, 1958.

A classic work on the experience of the divine in human life. It is a basic book for clarifying what religion is essentially all about, a foundation piece for grasping the meaning of religious experience.

ETHICS

Niebuhr, Reinhold. *An Interpretation of Christian Ethics.* Cleveland: World Publishing Company, 1963.

A classic work on the essential meaning of Christian ethics, what it does, what it can't do, and the complex ironies of democracy.

Illich, Ivan. *The Church, Change and Development.* Chicago: Urban Training Center Press, 1970.

An entirely different view from the Third World of the meaning of mission and doing good.

Schumacher, E.F. *Small Is Beautiful: Economics as if People Mattered.* New York: Harper and Row, 1973.

A recent examination of the morality of industrial development, economics, technology, and energy. A very humane examination of economic issues. Human well-being ranks above Gross National Product.

Swomley, John M., Jr. *Liberation Ethics.* New York: The Macmillan Company, 1972.

A clear, readable statement of the meaning of liberation theology for ethical behavior. Excellent statement of the power of nonviolence strategies for liberation.

Tillich, Paul. *Morality and Beyond.* New York: Harper and Row, 1963.

A basic work on morality and ethics with simple, though abstract, theological connections to his works in systematic theology.

King, Martin Luther, Jr. *Strength to Love.* New York: Harper and Row, 1963.

Sermons expressing how the power of love is necessary to overcome hatred. Words that explain his great nonviolent deeds.

EDUCATION

Freire, Paulo. *Pedagogy of the Oppressed.* Translated by Myra Bergman Ramos. New York: The Seabury Press, 1973.

Education is not neutral, it promotes liberation or pacification. This is Freire's basic work which gives a transforming perspective on education when it is used to liberate oppressed people.

Freire, Paulo. *Education for Critical Consciousness.* New York: The Seabury Press, 1973.

This volume is less complex than *Pedagogy* and gives a more practical, step-by-step approach to methods of conscientization in South America. It is very helpful in providing new lenses through which we can examine both education and our lives from the perspective of social structures.

O'Fahey, Sheila Moriarty, ed. *Deciding on the Human Use of Power.* Evansville, Illinois: Plover Books, 1975.

A well constructed study book on the meaning of using political power. Very readable and instructive, with case studies and suggested activities.

Russell, Letty M. *Christian Education in Mission.* Philadelphia: Westminster Press, 1967.

An early, practical guide to Christian education in the whole church in all of its activities. One of its major theses is that participatory learning in church functions from a global mission perspective.

Simon, Sidney B., Howe, Leland W., Kirschenbaum, Howard. *Values Clarifications: A Handbook of Practical Strategies for Teachers and Students.* New York: Hart Publishing Company, Inc., 1972.

This handbook offers very practical strategies or exercises that teachers can use in a classroom to raise value questions and move students to examine and re-examine their own values.

SOCIAL CHANGE

Alinsky, Saul D. *Rules for Radicals: A Practical Primer for Realistic Radicals.* New York: Random House, 1971.

Though this may be the "low road to morality," it does include critical wisdom for the activist. Don't try to change the system without letting Alinsky tell you what you are up against and what it costs to budge the system an inch.

Arnold, Joan. *Shalom Is . . . Whole Community.* Philadelphia: United Church Press, 1975.

A compact study of seven communities in which we all live. This theologian applies the Paulo Freire method of conscientization in demonstrating how we can lead more liberated lives.

Schaller, Lyle E. *The Change Agent, A Strategy of Innovative Leadership.* Nashville: Abingdon Press, 1972.

A general survey of social change tactics that gives an introductory overview for the change agent.

Sharp, Gene. *The Politics of Nonviolent Action.* Boston: Porter Sargent Publishers, 1973.

It's a catalog, it's a library, no, it's a compendium! This is the largest collection of tactics and historical records of nonviolent action ever pulled together and analyzed. It fills in all those gaps in the history books between the wars with hundreds of successful nonviolent campaigns.

Taylor, Richard K. *Economics and the Gospel.* Philadelphia: United Church Press, 1973.

An adult study book comparing the Bible to modern economic issues. Many suggestions are made for influencing the economic forces that confront us daily.

125